God's Good Earth in Crisis

God's Good Earth in Crisis

Liturgies of Lament

Compiled and Edited by
Anne and Jeffery Rowthorn
with the assistance of Marie Hause

Foreword by
Walter Brueggemann

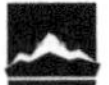 CASCADE *Books* • Eugene, Oregon

GOD'S GOOD EARTH IN CRISIS
Liturgies of Lament

Cascade Books
An Imprint of Wipf and Stock Publishers
199 W. 8th Ave., Suite 3
Eugene, OR 97401

www.wipfandstock.com

PAPERBACK ISBN: 978-1-6667-7953-0
HARDCOVER ISBN: 978-1-6667-7954-7
EBOOK ISBN: 978-1-6667-7955-4

Cataloguing-in-Publication data:

Names: Rowthorn, Anne W. [editor]. | Rowthorn, Jeffery [editor]. | Brueggemann, Walter [foreword writer].

Title: God's good earth in crisis : liturgies of lament / edited by Anne Rowthorn and Jeffery Rowthorn ; foreword by Walter Brueggemann.

Description: Eugene, OR: Cascade Books, 2024 | Includes bibliographical references and index.

Identifiers: ISBN 978-1-6667-7953-0 (paperback) | ISBN 978-1-6667-7954-7 (hardcover) | ISBN 978-1-6667-7955-4 (ebook)

Subjects: LCSH: Nature—Prayers and devotions. | Creation—Prayers and devotions. | Worship programs. | Liturgics. | Lament. | Public worship. | Nature—Religious aspects—Christianity. | Human ecology—Religious aspects—Christianity. | Creation—Religious aspects—Christianity.

Classification: BT695.5 R69 2024 (paperback) | BT695.5 (ebook)

VERSION NUMBER 05/17/24

For these dear friends and colleagues who meet the multitude of challenges posed by the Ecological Crisis through education, action, inspired congregational leadership, and poetry that touches the heartbeat of the universe—

Mary Evelyn Tucker and John Grim

Margaret Bullitt-Jonas

Talitha Arnold

Anita Louise Schell

Alla Renée Bozarth

and in memory of

Catherine de Vinck

. . . because, like Jimmy Carter, each could say, “I have one life and one chance to make it count for something. . . . My faith demands that I do whatever I can, wherever I am, as long as I can, with whatever I have, to try to make a difference.”

God is our refuge and strength, a very present help in trouble.
Therefore we will not fear, though the earth should change,
though the mountains shake in the heart of the sea,
though its waters roar and foam,
though the mountains tremble with its tumult.

—Psalm 46:1–3 (NRSVue)

A LITURGY OF LAMENT

Anne Wheeler Rowthorn

1939–2023

Anne oversaw the preparation of this book in all its parts except for the final proofing.
Then, when only that remained to be done, she died suddenly on July 28, 2023.

As a tribute to Anne, my beloved partner in life and work for sixty years, and her lifelong commitment to the well-being of God's good earth, it has been decided to bring the book to completion and publication.

May Anne Rest in Peace and in God's good time Rise in Glory.

+Jeffery Rowthorn
Co-compiler

CONTENTS

FOREWORD

The church in the West (including in the United States) has long been a triumphalist church. It has relied on a monopoly of authority, unquestioned certitude, and a reliable alliance with established power. Such a church, across the spectrum of religious communities, has been well settled, influential, and endowed with due deference. Such a church could afford to be buoyant and sure about its proclamation and confident in its claims. Specifically, such a church had no need to engage in lamentation, because it went mostly from victory to victory. As a result, the rich biblical tradition of lament has been blotted out from its wondrous potential.

Now all of that has changed in the Western church. The church is, accordingly, increasingly marginalized by the full force of secularism. Its mantras of certitude that could contain all of our vexations are no longer convincing to many people. The church has been able to live "from above" but now is resituated so that it must learn to live its life and bear its witness "from below," that is, from the midst of the incalculable disorder of our pained lives and our pained world. As the church has been required of late to become more fully "acquainted with infirmity," it has discovered that its long-running habits of confidence no longer prevail. Very slowly the church has come to an awareness that long before it can engage in *buoyant doxology* it must pause and linger in the practice of *honest unflinching lamentation* concerning a world filled with pain and concerning a God who is not as self-evident as in erstwhile sovereignty. The work of recovery of habits of lamentation has been very slow, both in terms of daring theological work "from below," and in terms of the necessary courage and imagination to engage the community in actual lament.

Given this drastic turn of affairs for the church, this book from the Rowthorns is as welcome as it is useful. The book does not linger long over theological formulation, but assumes the crises I have mentioned above, thus the term "crisis" in its title. The book rather focuses on actual resources for the pastoral liturgical practice of lamentation in living communities as an exercise in faithful truth-telling before God. Thus the book is an offer of rich pastoral resources from the treasure of church tradition and present testimony. In addition to a wide appeal to scripture, we get hymns, prayers, litanies, and commentary that reflect the courageous reality of lived, faithful experience that features many witnesses.

The book is an exercise in *truth-telling*. It does not dodge the hard issues we face in our world. It lingers a long time over what we might term "natural" crises that most often have human waywardness at their rootage. But it runs on toward more specifically social issues. It does not go very far into the destructive force of human fear, greed, and violence, but these markers of discordant living are everywhere present in this exposition. This rich collection of resources does not sugarcoat the distress in which we find ourselves.

The words of this book are unembarrassedly *God-addressed*. They do not simply invite us to the catharsis of truth-telling. The book is rather a mode of dialogical engagement with the Holy One. Thus the collection assumes the characteristic practice of prayer in which faithful people address the holy God, assume they can and will be heard, and anticipate a response from God. The words dwell in a tradition in which God is known and trusted to be a ready player.

As a result we can see that lamentation is not an act of resignation but *an exercise of hope*. As we tell our truth before God, we anticipate that our lament may move God to engage with us at the point of our common need. Thus, lament is an act of expectation that seeks to engage the Holy One in the troubles of our world that vex God's own creation.

This triad of *honest truth-telling, vigorous God-engagement*, and *resilient expectation* attests characteristic marks of Christian prayer and worship that are everywhere evident in this book. The Rowthorns are fortunately situated in the deep cadences of Anglican-Episcopal liturgic tradition. As a result they fully understand that durable laments can be readily transported from one crisis to another crisis only as they are not only honest, but that they are artfully crafted. Thus in this collection we can see laments voiced in disciplined imagination that sees clearly the world in front of us, and yet glimpses outside that world in order to see the new world of God's purpose that is crowding in upon us. Because I am rooted, by contrast, in a Free

Church tradition and have spent much time with biblical laments voiced in Jewish cadence, I would have wished for a more abrasive characterization of our social crises and for more urgent insistent imperative in our petition. But these wise church leaders know well what will work in the actual church, what will evoke good and lasting practice, and what will nourish faith beyond complacency and resignation.

On all counts this is a welcome, much-needed resource. I anticipate that it will have wide and blessed usage in the practice of the church that will enable the baptized community to move beyond the seductions of triumphalism and the certitudes of exceptionalism into the bodied life of the world where everything is at stake for the creator God. The book is a happy sequence to their previous compilation, *God's Good Earth: Praise and Prayer for Creation* (Liturgical Press, 2018) that will help to fund our imaginative practice in our own liturgical life. Readers of this book will be drawn to the powerful contemporaneity of the old traditions, a contemporaneity led by the Spirit beyond what the old writers themselves had understood. That Spirit that permeates these old readings is the same Spirit upon which the future of creation relies.

Walter Brueggemann
Columbia Theological Seminary

INTRODUCTION

Nobody knew more about lament than the slaves in Southern plantations. Nightly in their cabins, they sang out their sorrows, singing for comfort and solace, singing out of weariness and anger, hoping for freedom someday, but with no certainty as to when it would come.

> Nobody knows the trouble I've seen,
> Nobody knows but Jesus.
> Nobody knows the trouble I've seen,
> Glory hallelujah.
>
> Sometimes I'm up, sometimes I'm down,
> Oh, yes, Lord!
> Sometimes I'm almost to the ground,
> Oh, yes, Lord!
>
> Nobody knows the trouble I've seen,
> Nobody knows but Jesus.
> Nobody knows the trouble I've seen,
> Glory hallelujah.
>
> Although you see me going 'long so,
> Oh, yes, Lord!
> I have my troubles here below,
> Oh, yes, Lord!
>
> Nobody knows the trouble I've seen,
> Nobody knows but Jesus.
> Nobody knows the trouble I've seen,
> Glory hallelujah.[1]

Lament is always felt personally, whether it is experienced by an individual or by a group of people. It is the response to sudden catastrophe or to a jarring realization dawning on a large number of people. Lament is a cry of the heart, a call for help, a sense of drowning in sorrow, a deep hurt, a feeling of isolation and despair, an emotional response that focuses attention on the cause of the lament. Jeremiah, referring to the destruction of Jerusalem, writes, "My eyes are spent with weeping; my stomach churns; my bile is poured out on the ground because of the destruction of my people, because infants and babes faint in the streets of the city" (Lamentations 2:11 NRSVue). The Israelites in the wilderness complained to Moses and Aaron, "If only we had died by the hand of the LORD in the land of Egypt, when we sat by the pots of meat and ate our fill of bread, for you have brought us out into this wilderness to kill this whole assembly with hunger" (Exodus 16:3 NRSVue). Lament is a crying out in anger. Lament poses questions: "Why me?" "Why us?" Job asks, "Or why was I not buried like a stillborn child, like an infant that never sees the light?" (Job 3:16 NRSVue). He further asks, "Does God pervert justice? Or does the Almighty pervert the right?" (Job 8:3 NRSVue). The lamenter accuses God, asking God if we have been abandoned yet at the same time imploring God to rescue us.

Along with people all over the globe, we have spent almost three years immersed in lament. The year 2020 began as any other in northern climes—cold, dark, and snowy. But this year was going to be unique, and in retrospect we would discover just how unique the year would become.

When we arrived in Minnesota on January 20, 2019, the day the first Coronavirus case was reported in the USA, we thought nothing of it. We had come for a term as residential scholars at the Collegeville Institute on the campus of St. John's University and Abbey. It was wonderful being back in Collegeville, and we quickly renewed our friendships with Collegeville staff and friends in the monastic community. We bonded with new colleagues. This was our fourth visit and we had returned with many happy memories of our first time in 1981, when our children waited for the bus to take them to school in St. Cloud, sometimes in temperatures of 14 degrees below zero. The sky was crystal clear and the snow a pristine fresh linen-white. We were happy and immediately engaged in our research and writing projects, thrilled to be back to this very special place.

We could not have imagined how profoundly our lives would change in just a few short weeks. Starting out from Connecticut in January's chill, our greatest concern was avoiding snow storms and icy patches on interstate highways.

The new reality began to dawn. On January 31 the World Health Organization declared a "public health emergency of international concern." On

February 11, WHO gave the new coronavirus a name: COVID-19; February 26, the first case of "local transmission" was reported, followed by the first death in the USA on February 29. March 13, President Trump declared a national emergency. Two days later the Centers for Disease Control warned against gatherings larger than fifty people and urged elders aged sixty or older, along with people with health conditions, to "shelter in place."

On March 13 all students at St. John's were told to leave the campus and not to expect to return until the fall. The monks closed their services to outsiders, and they themselves sat in the choir with wide spaces between them, serving only the bread at celebrations of the Holy Eucharist.

On the first day of lockdown in Minnesota, March 28, we walked to the bridge over Interstate 94, a major, normally busy, upper-Midwest artery, and for ten minutes there was not a vehicle to be seen in either direction. It was as if the plague had struck, which indeed it had. On the first day of what was slated to be a two-week lockdown in Minnesota, the case count was 398 and four people had died.

The Collegeville Institute asked resident scholars to write a brief account of how the Coronavirus was affecting us. We wrote the following:

> In the evenings the dorms across the lake are dark; Flynntown is a ghost town. No longer do we hear the happy chatter of students. Our cottage has become a hermitage. Our only guests are squirrels and birds that come by the porch for snacks. Our daily routine remains mostly the same. One of us takes a sunrise hike and then we settle into the morning routine of reading, researching, and writing. After lunch we take another hike and a car ride with a fresh mug of tea. Evenings we play a card game, watch a movie, or read a recreational book.
>
> Here's what's different: We don't conclude an afternoon hike with a cup of coffee from a cafe; we order groceries on the Internet; we have had two Zoom prayer services; and we will also begin scholars' seminars on Zoom next week. Devoted mass-goers, we now watch the 5:00 mass live-streamed. Just hours before the library closed we checked out bags of novels and non-fiction light reading. We wait, we watch, we hope, we wonder. . . .

We watched the numbers of cases and deaths mount; we saw refrigerated trucks parked outside New York City hospitals waiting to receive the dead; harried nurses and doctors dressed in hazmat suits. In Rome on day twenty-one of lockdown our friend, Andrea, posted a picture of fifty hearses driving slowly by her apartment building. At our home in Connecticut, cases were beginning to swell, and the gym of Yale University was made into a field hospital. Our grandson, an EMT in a large Washington, DC, suburb, reported that almost all his calls were COVID-related and most of the patients were almost dead by the time his crew arrived.

Our children began to wonder how we were going to get home to safety, and we worried too. Should we jump in the car and drive straight to Connecticut, sleeping in it and bringing our own food? Should we wait it out until the summer, when travel would be safer? Our work at the Collegeville Institute suffered. We avoided crowds and stores, friends, and even the smallest gatherings. Thinking small towns were safer, with fewer people, we gloved and masked up and got our gas at Smith's Groceries and Gas in the tiny farming town of Holdingford, population 660.

In early April, word reached us that a dear friend, Dick, had died alone in a hospital in New London, Connecticut, after being there a week. Because of COVID, no family members could visit, not even Carole, his wife of sixty-seven years. She got the news of his passing over the phone. No parting hugs and kiss, no opportunity to say for one last time, "I love you." Carole endured alone while we struggled to comprehend her suffering, knowing it was being replicated again and again every day all over the nation and the world. This was when we wrote our first litany of lament, which is included in this book as a part of liturgy 13.

The reality of COVID in Minnesota hit hard in April. On April 24, 61,000 chickens were euthanized in Albany, a tiny agricultural town adjoining Collegeville. Thousands of gallons of milk were poured away at dairy farms. With restaurants and schools closed, chickens, milk, and eggs weren't needed. Infections and deaths mounted quickly. In Cold Spring, also close by, 1,100 workers at a turkey processing plant tested positive and were becoming ill and dying. In nearby Melrose, 750 workers tested positive; the same in a large pork processing plant further south in Worthington. We learned hard truths about the food supply system in the USA and about the extreme hardships of the food processing workers—tremendous cause for lament.

We visited Charlie's in Freeport, the café that was the model for Garrison Keillor's Chatterbox Café. Keillor would take a booth in the corner and listen to farmers' chatter and gossip, the prices of hogs and the local news. Whenever we are in Minnesota, we visit Charlie's for their delicious cinnamon rolls and fried walleye and small-town charm. But in late March, Charlie's was closed. Signs in the window in the shape of hearts read, "We

Are in This Together," and, "We Love You, Charlie's." The closing of Charlie's made us think of Anne's cousin, Fred, who had to close his popular bar and restaurant, the Rhumb Line, in Gloucester, Massachusetts. Laying off his loyal staff almost broke his heart. At the time, we said, "Truly our hearts ache for Fred, Charlie's workers, and the thousands of chefs, short order cooks, servers, dishwashers, bartenders, and cleaners. They are seriously hurting. We feel for them." More lament.

On April 27, our fifty-second day of social distancing, we were in a dark mood. The campus was quiet. We were locked out of the library and daily mass. Campus buildings were empty. Deaths were mounting. We wrote in our journal, "We dearly love Collegeville—one of us (Anne) has deep Minnesota roots, but it is not home. Tomorrow we should be leaving for Connecticut but instead we are waiting till it will be safer to travel. But when will that be?"

There were consolations. The St. John's campus is a lush 2,500 acre arboretum with abundant wildlife, hiking trails, and lakes; it's full of deer, ducks, geese, swans, turtles, and frogs. Every spring, the return of the loons with their haunting calls is awaited with fond anticipation. This year did not disappoint, and in fact, we felt supported, uplifted, and inspired by the beauty all around us. At least in this small part of the world, the cycles of nature seemed normal and dependable. We shared culinary treats among our community of scholars in the Collegeville Institute; we worshiped together online; and when the weather warmed up, we had socially distanced pizza parties outside. Carla, an unfailingly kind Institute staffer, checked to see if we needed anything and picked up groceries for us in town. Our friend, Brother Walter, brought us bags full of watercress he'd picked and bottles of maple syrup from the sugar maple grove. Our mass buddy, a Collegeville neighbor, Paul, brought us Easter treats of ham, wine, decorated eggs, and a charming homemade Easter card. When the supermarkets ran out of yeast, Brother Aelred taught us how to make a delicious sourdough bread, which doesn't require yeast.

On May 24, with nearly 100,000 Americans dead from COVID, the *New York Times* listed all their names under the heading, "They are not simply names on a list. They were us."

The very next day—May 25—George Floyd was savagely killed on a Minneapolis street, sending shock waves throughout the nation and the world and occasioning intense anger and a fresh look at the pervasive racism afflicting this country. Floyd's murder, just seventy-five miles away from us in Minneapolis, was a jolt that put our personal worries in perspective. How long, O Lord, how long will it be till it's safe for a black man to go to a convenience store and drive home unimpeded?

The death of George Floyd was a watershed moment. The nation—already traumatized by COVID—saw the uncovering of our political, class, and economic divides and the unleashing of fury, rage, and division. Masked and unmasked people representing all points of view took to the streets to demonstrate their feelings and frustrations.

May 11, the day of St. John's University graduation, the campus was cloudy, dark, and cold. Festive flags floated outside the Abbey church, representing the countries of the graduates. The signboard at the entrance of the campus read, "Congratulations Class of 2020," but there was nary a graduate in sight to see it. How many disappointed students, proud parents, and grandparents in colleges and universities across the nation were quiet and alone on what should have been a grand festival day of celebration?

We got home on June 15, socially distancing even from family and close friends. Over the summer, wildfires raged in the American West; record high summer temperatures and heat waves abounded all over the world. As fall approached, COVID cases increased. Students remained at home, learning online, causing hardships for parents and caregivers. College towns were deserted. Thanksgiving passed without family members and friends gathering in large numbers to share the table. Before Christmas, two more friends died of COVID; one of them, Dottie, was Anne's friend from time shared as teenagers on a South Dakota Indian reservation. Her death cut Anne to the quick.

Gun violence continued unabated. There was social unrest. The unthinkable happened and our nation's Capitol was stormed by a violent mob on the Feast of the Epiphany. Where was the balm in Gilead, or in Atlanta, Boulder, Washington, DC, or Indianapolis?

The pandemic, gun violence, deep social divides and social unrest, violence against people of color—all of these played out, and continue to do so, against the pervasive backdrop of the climate crisis. Floods, drought, extreme heat, rising sea levels, ocean acidification, famine, wildfires continue unabated. These are more than ample cause for lament.

We had become utterly preoccupied with lament. It was difficult to concentrate on anything else. While we were in Minnesota, we wrote a daily online journal we called the "Collegeville Journal." It was a means of attempting to come to terms with the collective worldwide trauma in which we were all engaged. We wrote two litanies of lament and we began to look at lament biblically and theologically.

According to the biblical scholar Claus Westermann, whose seminal work on lament, *Praise and Lament in the Psalms*, has been reprinted many times, lament in the Psalms, and in the Bible, generally, takes two forms: the lament of the individual, and the lament of the people, the community.

THE LAMENT OF THE INDIVIDUAL

The ten-year-old boy on a school vacation day helps his father, a tree surgeon, and tragically gets pulled into the wood-chipper. The life of the family is changed in the instant they are hit by a drunk driver while walking from their home to a Sunday evening church service. The eight-year-old daughter is killed, the mother made a paraplegic, the father and six-year-old son left grieving. The single mother's only two children are killed together in a single car accident on Easter Sunday morning. A stroke leaves the man speechless and paralyzed a week after he and his wife celebrate their fortieth wedding anniversary in Paris. The vibrant, healthy mother of three teenagers develops an aggressive brain tumor that seeps life out of her in an agonizing descent into death. The graduate student dives into the flood-swollen Missouri River to rescue a ten-year-old, gets him to shore, then dies of a heart attack. The only child, dearly beloved adopted daughter of a middle-aged couple, gets pulled to her death off the rocks in a fierce storm at Acadia National Park. The young man in his twenties who was just beginning to get his life together has an accidental overdose. The thirty-two-year-old daughter of a family member, finally happy with a good job and a host of friends after a hard childhood, acquires a rare and deadly cancer, becomes increasingly ill, and dies nine months later. We ask ourselves "Why?" Why are these young people taken at the prime of their lives? Why her? Why them? Why at this time? How about the survivors? These are what Westermann would term individual laments.

THE LAMENT OF THE PEOPLE

Fields are dry and cracked. No rain is in sight; the drought has continued twenty years. Farmers are forced out, the ground withers, animals die; agriculture comes to a halt. The sun is relentless; temperatures rise. Wildlife and plants die off; wildfires break out, turning whole communities into infernos.

The wind blows, spreading the fires. Rains pour incessantly, swelling rivers, and breaching dams. Tectonic plates shift; the ground shakes and trembles, bringing down tall buildings and tin-roofed houses, opening fissures in interstate highways. Hurricanes slam against coastlines; tsunamis obliterate coastal villages, sweeping away people and property. Rising sea levels force evacuations from island nations and low-lying coastlines. Waves sweep over nuclear reactors, dispersing nuclear material to the sea. The hulls of oil tankers break and thousands of gallons of crude oil contaminate the ocean and coasts. Oil pipelines break, polluting precious drinking water. The social fabric gets strained and breaks. People take to the streets and even to the halls of the US Capitol. Gun sales abound, triggers are pulled, innocents are killed. Racism in all its forms rears its ugly face and gun-toting vigilantes parade the streets. A pandemic starts in one distant corner of the globe and a year later every nation on earth is affected, with millions dead, especially the most vulnerable—the elderly, people of color, people living and working in crowded conditions. Why are the people suffering? How has this happened? Where is justice? Will we have to evacuate? How long will we be displaced? How will we bury our dead? Will life as we knew it ever return? Old Testament scholar Walter Brueggemann has said,

> [Communal psalms] permit us to remember that we are indeed public citizens and have an immediate, direct, and personal stake in public events. The recovery of this mode of psalmic prayer may be important if we are to overcome our general religious abdication of public issues and the malaise of indifference and apathy that comes with the abdication.[2]

Laments of this sort are laments of the people, and these are the laments we are addressing in this book.

THE LAMENTS OF ENSLAVED PEOPLE

The most obvious example of lament of the people comes from the slave cabins and camps of Southern plantations. Slaves had brought with them their own religious practices from Africa, which, when melded with Christianity, produced a rich liturgy of singing, praying, dancing, drumming, preaching in the form of call and response. Through nightly meetings, slaves drew strength from each other as they poured out their sorrows. These gatherings were essential to their survival. As Donna M. Cox, music professor at the University of Dayton, said, "In order to survive emotionally, resilience was critical. In the spirituals slaves sang out of their struggle, weariness, loneliness, sorrow, hope and their determination to find a new and better life."[3] And so they sang—"Nobody knows the trouble I've seen, nobody but Jesus," "Steal away, steal away, steal away to Jesus," "Sometimes I feel like a motherless child," "Deep River, my home is over Jordan. . . . O don't you want to go to that promised land where all is peace?"

Frederick Douglass described the lament of the slaves singing in their camps:

> [T]hey were tones loud, long, and deep; they breathed the prayer and complaint of souls boiling over with the bitterest anguish. Every tone was a testimony against slavery, and a prayer to God for deliverance from chains. . . . Slaves sing most when they are most unhappy. The songs of the slave represent the sorrows of his heart; and he is relieved by them, only as an aching heart is relieved by its tears.[4]

The liturgies of the slave communities, finally, pointed to hope in the struggles of the people: hope for freedom, hope for heaven if freedom didn't come soon enough. In the process, they gave to the world a magnificent treasury of poignant heartfelt music and a model in our time for confronting our sorrows liturgically.

REVIVING THE LANGUAGE OF LAMENT IN WORSHIP

Back home, staying home and isolating ourselves, we searched for liturgies of lament. There are prayers of individual lament and consolation, prayers focusing on individual suffering—death in the family, illness, bereavement, and such—and churches are very good at addressing these laments. But as far as the liturgical expression of communal lament is concerned—that is, the lament of the people—we came up empty in our search for complete services addressing particular aspects of lament, apart from the spirituals of the slave communities.

Biblical scholars, particularly Song-Chan Rah, Walter Brueggemann, and Claus Westermann, have contributed to the scholarship of lament, and for the most part they conclude that lament has largely dropped out of liturgical expression in favor of praise and thanksgiving. Brueggemann asks the question:

> What happens when appreciation of lament as a form of speech and faith is lost, as I think is largely lost in contemporary usage? What happens when the speech forms that redress power distribution have been silenced and eliminated? The answer, I believe, is that a theological monopoly is reinforced, docility and submissiveness are engendered. . . . [L]ament makes an assertion about God: that this dangerous, available God matters in *every* dimension of life. Where God's dangerous availability is lost because we fail to carry on our part of the difficult conversation, where God's vulnerability and passion are removed from our speech, we are consigned to anxiety and despair, and the world as we now have it becomes absolutized.[5]

Given the erosion of a broad sense of community and responsibility in public life, Brueggemann places the problem in a wider context:

> We have little experiential counterpart to the communal laments. Given our privatistic inclination, we do not often think about public disasters as concerns for prayer life. If we do, we treat them as somehow a lesser item. We have nearly lost our capacity to think theologically about public issues and public problems. Even more, we have lost our capacity to practice prayer in relationship to public events.[6]

Others will examine the reasons why communal lament is treated so thinly in our day. Our aim has been to educate ourselves. We steeped ourselves in the biblical themes of lament, especially the psalms of lament; the books of Job, Jeremiah, and Lamentation; and elsewhere throughout Hebrew scripture. Lament is the language of suffering, and our spiritual forebears knew this well and addressed it: the laments of Cain, Samson, Job, Moses; the laments of the Israelites in exile; the laments of the people of Jerusalem after being invaded by the Babylonian army. And perhaps the most poignant lament of all, Jesus's final words on the cross, "My God, my God, why have you forsaken me?" (Matthew 27:46 NRSVue, taken from Psalm 22:2). Fuller Seminary professor Soong-Chan Rah says in his book *Prophetic Lament*,

> As the people of God recount their suffering and their painful history, they call out to God . . . and ask many of the same questions we ask today: Where is our hope even in the midst of suffering and death? Can we see God in all circumstances of life? Does our understanding of a historical reality impact our current reality?[7]

We read, pondered, and prayed, and almost spontaneously we began compiling a collection of liturgies addressing communal lament. Over the second long winter of COVID we became even more convinced of the utter necessity for the churches and citizens everywhere, of every religion and none, to make prayer for the laments of our planet the top priority. Facing up to our lament over the disastrous state of Planet Earth and all her interrelated people, animals, plants, soils, seas, and skies is an essential first step in Earth's restoration and the recovery of hope and joy in all that lives.

Theologian and social ethicist Emilie M. Townes stresses the importance, as she says, of "naming the hot mess" we are in, confessing that we cannot necessarily right the wrongs that affect us, except by standing up, digging in and facing reality. . . .

> We face the tough times of our day with fresh energy and urgency that remind us that we stand on the frontlines of hope. This hope is neither sentimental nor vapid. It does not give up on God or us. Hope refuses to believe that evil and suffering and sorrow and hatred are God's final words to us in a world that is a spinning top of war and violence. This hope believes and guides us to another way in which we are made whole—the power of the common good shaping our lives and that of countless others on the highway to salvation.[8]

As of this writing, worldwide deaths from COVID have almost reached the seven million mark. Tonga has been hit by a catastrophic earthquake and resulting tsunami. Last summer, one-third of Pakistan was under water in what was described as an "Apocalyptic Crisis." Right now, Australia is enduring record-making temperatures of 123 degrees and multiple bushfires. China is experiencing a drought that is drying up its major rivers and gravely reducing its hydroelectric power. Arctic permafrost is melting, threatening the survival of native villages and contributing to sea-level rising. In North America we experienced another summer of heat waves, droughts, wildfires, hurricanes and floods, and the playing out of COVID variants. Plant and animal species of all kinds are on the edge of extinction. A war is raging in Ukraine. Americans are seeing our political system coming apart, social and economic divisions deepening, and gun violence and suicides increasing, especially among children and young adults. The whole world is in an existential crisis and people are losing hope.

There are no easy answers to every cause of lament, and there is no promise that amelioration will come quickly, but we have become convinced that addressing our laments liturgically in our communities of faith would be a positive step forward. Liturgy at its best has the power to transform the community of the faithful by evoking our best and raising awareness. Addressing lament through worship opens up the potential to rebalance the polarities of thanksgiving and joy with sorrow and lament, thereby enriching and deepening corporate worship. It builds up strength and resilience, counters isolation, offers hope and sometimes even joy. Lament for *our own suffering community* lends itself to shared compassion and solidarity with each other; lament *on behalf of others* suffering tragedies arouses our consciousness and our willingness to reach out in love and action. Margaret Bullitt-Jonas, Missioner for Creation Care for the Episcopal Diocese of Western Massachusetts and the Southern New England Conference of the United Church of Christ, says,

> What would it be like—how might it empower us—if we took time in worship services . . . to lament species that have gone extinct, forests that have burned, or reservoirs that have run dry? Daring to lament together allows us to feel our deep longing for healing and reconciliation and to experience the God who weeps with us. Daring to lament together protects our human capacity to feel our emotional responses without being overwhelmed. And it allows our emotions to become a source of energy for constructive action to address the emergency.[9]

Underneath all of our laments, there remains an enduring sense of hope, relying on God who we know is with us even in the saddest and most desperate of times. "The steadfast love of God never ceases, God's mercies never come to an end; they are new every morning; great is your faithfulness" (Lamentations 3:22–23, adapted).

ABOUT THIS BOOK AND HOW TO USE IT

This book grew out of our deeply felt anguish and sense of loss, immediately occasioned by our response to the COVID-19 pandemic. We saw COVID as one of many causes of the lament we had been carrying in our minds and in our hearts, and all against the backdrop of the rapidly deteriorating state of our beloved Planet Earth. In our book *God's Good Earth: Praise and Prayer for Creation*, we addressed certain aspects of lament under the category entitled "The Whole Creation Groaning in Travail." The topics included exploitation of the earth, global warming, climate change, forgotten people, poverty, hunger, migrants, violence, and the victims of war.

With this volume, we focus more immediately on the issue of lament in its most usual forms, especially the lament experienced by communities of people. To start with, we conducted our research for content in libraries, but we quickly found that most of the prayers and litanies we wanted for inclusion in this book have not yet made it into print. We thus turned to the internet and found excellent material. Many prayers in their original form focus on a specific urgent issue such as wildfire in Paradise, California, or nuclear meltdown in Fukushima, Japan. We have adapted these sources for general use and in some cases designed litanies from prayers; when pieces have been adapted, this is indicated by the inclusion of "alt." in the citation. We also wrote our own prayers and litanies when other sources were not available. A few prayers have been drawn from printed prayer collections and the worship books of various denominations.

A key component of this project has been the participation of twelve partner parishes drawn from the diversity of congregations across the nation. Partner parishes tested the liturgies and offered their feedback. Due to their generous contributions, these liturgies reflect the actual experiences of the People of God and make this a truly communal project.

With the exception of the concluding liturgy, each liturgy is a complete service of worship focused on a specific theme. They all follow the same pattern, with these elements: introduction, beginning prayers, psalm or canticle, scripture reading, litany, reflection, concluding prayers, hymn, and a benediction. The services may be supplemented by the addition of a processional hymn. Free prayer, prayers of the community, and the Lord's Prayer may be added after the second section of prayers before the hymn. The services may also include the celebration of the Eucharist. To do so, we suggest: adding a passage from one of the Gospels; adding a confession; offering bread and wine according to the Eucharistic practice of your denomination; then ending with the hymn and benediction from this book.

God's Good Earth in Crisis may also be used as an anthology of prayers and litanies, and we encourage worship leaders to freely pick and choose selections appropriate to the crisis at hand. New crises will inevitably arise, calling for new occasions for prayers of lament. When that happens, we hope you will adapt resources in this book that speak to the moment. For example, the chapters "Petroleum Pipelines," "Ocean Oil Spills," and "Meltdown" could be adapted to accommodate oil spills on land, chemical leaks, and industrial accidents. We hope that you will be creative and craft new liturgies as needs arise.

A short note is in order about the occasional appearance of the holy Name of God, YHWH, in the liturgies. Y H W H are the consonants of the divine Name, sometimes referred to as the Tetragrammaton. Jews consider God's Name so holy that they do not utter it. So when YHWH is written in the sacred text they will substitute the title Adonai (meaning "Lord") in their reading. We invite you to do the same. In other words, when YHWH is *written*, we invite you to *say* "Adonai."

God's Good Earth in Crisis is offered to worship leaders, small groups, and congregations in the conviction that worship is the most powerful means the Holy Spirit uses to equip and transform us to live faithful lives serving God and caring for God's holy people and sacred Earth. We live in the belief that such a transformation is not only possible but essential in reviving God's good earth.

Anne Rowthorn and Jeffery Rowthorn

1. EXTREME HEAT

Earth's temperature is rising and the entire planet is suffering from a punishing fever. The world's thermostat must be turned down immediately so that people and animals, plants, soils, seas, and sky may live and thrive.

The more we heat up the planet, the more it costs all of us, not just in money, but in colossal famines, displacements, deaths, and species extinctions, as well as in the loss of some of the things that make this planet a blue-green jewel, including its specialized habitats from the melting Arctic to bleaching coral reefs. (*Rebecca Solnit*)[10]

PRAYERS

Eternal God, you are the power that created the universe, the energy that fires everything, the strength that sustains the world. Eternal Father, you are the love that encircles us, the grace that enables us, the truth that enlightens us. Eternal Savior, you are the glory of the cross of Christ, the hope of the resurrection, the life of the Holy Spirit. God of love, power, and glory: we praise you. ***Amen***. (*Anne Knighton*)[11]

God of all creation, we cry out to you. The sun's heat is unrelenting. The land is our hurting partner; she is hot, she is thirsty, she is cracked and dry. Lord of the rains, you weep for creation when she is hurt. Lord of life, you weep with us in our loss, our despair, our hunger and thirst. Hear the cries of our heart, O God, and give us your Spirit to sustain us in this extreme heat.

Lord, some livestock are dying, others languish for lack of feed; stir up those who have resources to share in their abundance, that the creatures in our care may not suffer.

Lord, great economic stress hovers over us. Protect our families, all our loved ones, our communities from the ravages of this hot dry season. Send your Holy Spirit to draw us to the wellspring of life and hope where despair and hopelessness are known no more. We pray that you will be with us in this time of our great need. ***Amen.*** (*Bill Harder and the Evangelical Lutheran Church in Canada Synod of Alberta and the Territories)*[12]

CANTICLE ISAIAH 35:1–10

The wilderness and the parched land will exult;
    the Arabah will rejoice and bloom;
Like a crocus it shall bloom abundantly,
    and rejoice with joyful song.

The glory of Lebanon will be given to it,
    the splendor of Carmel and Sharon;
they will see the glory of the LORD,
    the splendor of our God.

Strengthen the hands that are feeble,
    make firm knees that are weak,
Say to the fearful of heart:
    Be strong, do not fear!

Here is your God,
    he comes with vindication;
With divine recompense
    he comes to save you.

Then the eyes of the blind shall see,
    and the ears of the deaf be opened;
Then the lame shall leap like a stag,
    and the mute tongue sing for joy.

For waters shall burst forth in the wilderness,
    and streams in the Arabah.

The burning sands will become pools,
and the thirsty ground, springs of water;
The abode where jackals crouch
will be a marsh for the reed and papyrus.

A highway will be there,
called the holy way.

No one unclean may pass over it,
but it will be for his people;
no traveler, not even fools, shall go astray on it.

No lion shall be there,
nor any beast of prey approach,
nor be found,
but there redeemed shall walk.

And the ransomed of the LORD shall return,
and enter Zion singing,
crowned with everlasting joy;

They meet with joy and gladness,
sorrow and mourning flee away![13]

SCRIPTURE LAMENTATIONS 4:2–5, 9, 11–14, 17

The precious children of Zion,
worth their weight in fine gold—
how they are reckoned as earthen pots,
the work of a potter's hands!

Even the jackals offer the breast
and nurse their young,
but my people has become cruel,
like the ostriches in the wilderness.

The tongue of the infant sticks
to the roof of its mouth for thirst;
the children beg for food,
but there is nothing for them.

Those who feasted on delicacies
    perish in the streets;
those who were brought up in purple
    cling to ash heaps. . . .

Happier were those pierced by the sword
    than those pierced by hunger,
whose life drains away, deprived
    of the produce of the field. . . .

The LORD gave full vent to his wrath;
    he poured out his hot anger,
and kindled a fire in Zion
    that consumed its foundations.

The kings of the earth did not believe,
    nor did any of the inhabitants of the world,
that foe or enemy could enter
    the gates of Jerusalem.

It was for the sins of her prophets
    and the iniquities of her priests,
who shed the blood of the righteous
    in her midst.

Blindly they wandered through the streets,
    so defiled with blood
that no one was able
    to touch their garments. . . .

Our eyes failed, ever watching
    vainly for help;
we were watching eagerly
    for a nation that could not save. (*NRSVue*)

LITANY ANNE ROWTHORN

Someone's suffering from extreme heat, Lord; someone somewhere in the world where it's summer. That someone is millions and millions of your holy people who live and work and sleep and die in heat too hot for human bodies, too hot for many animals and plants. They are our brothers and sisters, our mothers and fathers, aunts and uncles, our friends and neighbors—all precious people and plants and animals beloved by the holy God of the universe—

Good God, stand with them.

From the Punjab to northern Rajasthan to Phoenix and Los Angeles; from Kuala Lumpur to Kansas City; from California's Central Valley and the wheat fields of Kansas to the grasslands of Ukraine and Kazakhstan—farmers, growers, pickers of crops are suffering heat exhaustion, dehydration and sunstroke—

Good God, stand with them.

Wheat, corn, sugar beets, rice, cotton and beans wither, languish and die in the baking heat—

Good God, stand with them.

For bats and bears, cattle, caribou, kookaburras and chickens, bees and birds of the air enduring extreme heat—

Good God, stand with them.

For fields and pastures, grasslands and prairies and for the sun-baked soil—

Good God, stand with them.

For builders of the world's roads and highways struggling in insufferable heat—

Good God, stand with them.

Construction workers and roofers, lawn-care laborers, gardeners, and police on the beat—

Good God, stand with them.

From the Mississippi Delta to the pueblos of Arizona and New Mexico where people have no air conditioning—

Good God, stand with them.

For the elderly and the poor living in cramped city apartments where hardly a whiff of fresh air blows through—

Good God, stand with them.

Help us to appreciate that the bread we eat from the blisteringly hot fields, is the bread of suffering, and arouse our consciences to work for safe conditions for farmers and pickers and for all whose work is outside on blistering summer days—

Good God, stand with them and arouse us to action on their behalf.[14]

REFLECTION KATHY BAUGHMAN McLEOD

People are dying from heat and heat waves, and we don't really know it or fully understand it. It's called a "silent killer," because we record these illnesses and deaths as something else—like kidney failure or heart attack. Heat is killing more people in the US than floods and hurricanes combined, and the numbers are still seriously deflated. We also know that in the US heat disproportionately affects low-income and black and brown communities. . . . Low-income areas tend to be treeless, concrete-filled neighborhoods that are significantly hotter than adjacent, leafy, wealthier neighborhoods. . . .

Heat is the mothership of climate risk—it exacerbates hurricanes driven by warmer air and warmer water, drought and desertification, devastating and cataclysmic wildfires, food insecurity, water shortages, increased violence, and immense economic loss. And it's not just extreme heat. It's the slow-roasting increased nighttime temperatures that don't allow the body to cool down and repair itself. We are literally cooking ourselves. And, during the day, when temperatures are most dangerous, outdoor workers are severely exposed—think of all the farmworkers and delivery drivers out there. . . .[15]

Kathy Baughman McLeod is the senior vice president and director of the Adrienne Arsht-Rockefeller Foundation at the Atlantic Council, where she is a leader of the Extreme Heat Resilience Alliance. To draw attention to the rising scourge of deadly heat waves, the group has proposed naming heat waves in the same way that we name hurricanes in order to focus public attention on them.

PRAYERS

Holy God of earth, wind, heat, and fire: we lift up to you all nations and people suffering in unrelenting, extreme heat; for people living in cities whose sidewalks are blisteringly hot and whose streets are melting; for all who lack fans, ventilation, and air conditioning, especially the elderly and vulnerable, and workers struggling under adverse conditions. We pray for all aid workers and essential workers and those whose work is outside in the heat of the noonday sun. We pray especially for all who have lost family and friends in this heat wave. Be present to them and comfort them in their grief. We implore you to send refreshing breezes and cooler temperatures. All this we ask in your name, Jesus, knowing that you hear our prayers and are close to the broken-hearted. ***Amen.*** *(Anne Rowthorn)*[16]

God of opportunity and change, praise to you for giving us life at this critical time. As our horizons extend, keep us loyal to our past; as our dangers increase, help us to prepare for the future; keep us trusting and hopeful, ready to recognize your kingdom as it comes. ***Amen.*** *(The Church of the Province of New Zealand)*[17]

HYMN NORMAN HABEL

1. Wise up, wise up, all Christians
whose eyes are heaven bound;
God made us first in Eden
to serve and love the ground,
to work with God the Gard'ner
whose breath in ev'ry thing
brings life and hope and blessing
and makes our planet sing.

2. Be wise, be wise, like Joseph,
before those years of drought,
the curse of global warming
turns human faith to doubt.
Plan now to feed the hungry,
a flood of refugees,
and share our garden planet
with ev'ry life in need.

3. Connect with Christ the healer
whose love fills land and sea,
that breathing, pulsing presence
in soil and stream and tree.
Unite with Christ in healing
the wounds of Planet Earth
until creation's groaning
becomes a song of birth.[18]

Tune: MUNICH, 7.6.7.6 D

Take courage; be confident and strong; go where you must go, do what you must do. Shed tears, endure sorrow, live with loneliness. Put your hope in the risen Christ, who leads us through death to resurrection and eternal joy. ***Amen.*** *(Alan Gaunt)*[19]

2. DROUGHT

The formula is simple: soil, sun, and water in correct proportions. In the absence of rain, soils dry up; plants wither; people hunger and thirst; winds blow over parched fields, and more and more land disintegrates into desertification.

For I will pour water on the thirsty land and streams on the dry ground . . . (*Isaiah 44:3a NRSVue)*

PRAYERS

God of earth and sky, land and seas: break open the vault of heaven and pour rain upon the dry lands. May every country and all peoples on earth who suffer from drought be drenched in rain until the land is quenched and the ditches overflow. May we dance in the rain as we sing praise to you for your provision. ***Amen.*** *(Bill Harder and the Evangelical Lutheran Church in Canada Synod of Alberta and the Territories)*[20]

O God, we pray for those places in the world where people suffer from extreme climactic conditions: places of intense cold, and heat and drought, places of great hardship and privation, where man, woman, and beast are constantly endangered by the elements and the environment. We give thanks for all that sustains and helps them, and pray that such may be multiplied in the hands of Jesus Christ. ***Amen.*** (*World Council of Churches)*[21]

O holy God, you created our earth to nourish us and give us life, and Jesus told us to ask and it will be given to us. We ask now in faith, hope, and love that you look with favor on our drought-stricken land, our starving animals and failing produce. Sustain, strengthen, and give new heart to our farmers and all those affected by this drought. In your loving providence send abundant rain soon and renew the faith of your people and the face of our land. We make this prayer with many, through Jesus Christ who gives new life to all living things. ***Amen.*** *(Columba Macbeth-Green)*[22]

CANTICLE JEREMIAH 14:1–6, 9B

The word of the LORD that came to Jeremiah concerning the drought:

Judah mourns,
her gates are lifeless;
They are bowed to the ground,
and the outcry of Jerusalem goes up.

The nobles send their servants for water,
but when they come to the cisterns
They find no water
and return with empty jars.

Confounded, despairing, they cover their heads
because of the ruined soil;

Because there is no rain in the land
the farmers are confounded; they cover their heads.

Even the doe in the field deserts her young
because there is no grass.

The wild donkeys stand on the bare heights,
gasping for breath like jackals;
Their eyes grow dim;
there is no grass. . . .

You are in our midst, LORD,
your name we bear:
do not forsake us![23]

2. Drought

SCRIPTURE ISAIAH 41:10, 13, 14B, 17–20

. . . do not fear, for I am with you;
do not be afraid, for I am your God;
I will strengthen you; I will help you;
I will uphold you with my victorious right hand. . . .

For I, the LORD your God,
hold your right hand;
it is I who say to you, "Do not fear,
I will help you." . . .

I will help you, says the LORD;
your Redeemer is the Holy One of Israel. . . .

When the poor and needy seek water,
and there is none,
and their tongue is parched with thirst,
I the LORD will answer them,
I the God of Israel will not forsake them.
I will open rivers on the bare heights
and fountains in the midst of the valleys;
I will make the wilderness a pool of water
and the dry land springs of water.
I will put in the wilderness the cedar,
the acacia, the myrtle, and the olive;
I will set in the desert the cypress,
the plane and the pine together,
so that all may see and know,
all may consider and understand,
that the hand of the LORD has done this,
the Holy One of Israel has created it. (*NRSVue*)

LITANY SIMON HANSFORD

We pray for the land. We hear the promise you have spoken to Isaiah of the refreshment of the creation; of water in the desert, of renewal for the land, of hope, of life.

O loving God, hear our prayer.

We name our simple need—rain for our thirsty land. Our tanks and dams are nearly empty, like our hopes for this season.

O loving God, hear our prayer.

Please, loving God, bring us rain to renew the ground, to bring some chance of feed, to bring the possibility of some reward to those who have toiled so hard. We turn to you in faith and hope.

O loving God, hear our prayer.

We pray for all those whose lives are under the shadow of drought.

O loving God, hear our prayer.

We think first of those who work with the land, for farmers and their families, for those who rely upon the land for their life and relationships.

O loving God, hear our prayer.

We pray for contractors, merchants, and truck drivers, for rural counselors and support workers, for all our rural community.

O loving God, hear our prayer.

May the refreshment of your Spirit, present in miraculous and truly human ways, be with all of us as we move forward into the days ahead.

O loving God, hear our prayer.

We pray for justice; for fair prices for our stock and our wool and our crops. We pray for governments, banks, and corporations that they may be driven by a sense of community, justice, and compassion.

O loving God, hear our prayer.

We pray for each other. Keep us aware of the needs of those around us: for those who are struggling, who are grieving, who are ill, who are dying.

O loving God, hear our prayer.

Let us see the miracle of healing for the land and the restoration of hope.

O loving God, hear our prayer. We offer all these prayers in the name of Jesus.[24]

2. Drought

REFLECTION CAROLINE HENDERSON

Wearing our shade hats, with handkerchiefs tied over our faces and vaseline in our nostrils, we have been trying to rescue our home from the accumulations of wind-blown dust which penetrates wherever air can go. It is an almost hopeless task, for there is rarely a day when at some time the dust clouds do not roll over. "Visibility" approaches zero and everything is covered again with a silt-like deposit which may vary in depth from a film to actual ripples on the kitchen floor. I keep oiled cloths on the window sills and between the upper and lower sashes. . . .

Early in May, with no more grass or even weeds on our 640 acres than your kitchen floor, and even the scanty remnants of dried grasses from last year cut off and blown away, we decided, like most of our neighbors, to ship our cattle to grass in the central part of the state. . . . [O]n a sixty-mile trip yesterday to procure tractor repairs we saw many pitiful reminders of broken hopes and apparently wasted effort. Little abandoned homes where people had drilled deep wells for the precious water, had set trees and vines, built reservoirs, and fenced in gardens—with everything now walled in or half buried by banks of drifted soil—told a painful story of loss and disappointment. . . .

Naturally you will wonder why we stay where conditions are so extremely disheartening. Why not pick up and leave as so many others have done? . . . We may *have* to leave. . . . But I think I can never go willingly or without pain that as yet seems unendurable. . . . We long for the garden and little chickens, the trees and birds and wild flowers of the years gone by. Perhaps if we do our part these good things may return some day, for others if not for ourselves.[25]

Caroline Henderson, a farmer in Oklahoma, wrote a series of letters for The Atlantic *describing life during the Dust Bowl of the 1930s. Years of drought left the land ravaged, forcing thousands of farm families to flee. It was the largest mass movement of people within the United States. The heartbreak of people fleeing their homelands because of adverse climactic conditions continues.*

PRAYERS

Hear us, O Lord, as we remember before you all in the farming community; all who fear for the continuation of their livelihood or employment; all who must bear the loss of years of anxious toil and the suffering of creatures entrusted to their charge; all in doubt about the future for themselves and their families and who feel themselves isolated and alone. Uplift those that are cast down, O Lord, and cheer with hope all the discouraged: uphold their faith, raise up helpers in their need and grant that they may ever find peace, healing, and hope. Through Jesus Christ we pray. ***Amen.*** *(Arthur Rank Centre)*[26]

Creating God, today we pray for your blessing upon the land, and upon all whose life depends on it. We pray for farmers and ranchers, for abundant harvests and healthy herds. We acknowledge the fragility of all life and we pray for ourselves as your people, that we might nurture and respect all creation. Free us from harmful attitudes and actions towards the land, the crops, and animals; free us from despair in times of drought and flood; free us from wastefulness and greed in times of plenty. May our farming and ranching this season reflect awareness of our bonds with the earth, now and for generations yet to come. ***Amen.*** *(Author unknown)*[27]

HYMN ISAAC WATTS

1. O God, our help in ages past,
   our hope for years to come,
   our shelter from the stormy blast,
   and our eternal home;

2. Under the shadow of your throne
   your saints have dwelt secure.
   Sufficient is your arm alone,
   and our defense is sure.

3. Before the hills in order stood,
   or earth received its frame,
   from everlasting you are God,
   to endless years the same.

4. A thousand ages in your sight
   are like an evening gone,
   short as the watch that ends the night
   before the rising sun.

5. Time, like an ever-rolling stream,
   soon bears us all away.
   We fly forgotten, as a dream
   dies at the opening day.

6. O God, our help in ages past,
   our hope for years to come,
   still be our guard while troubles last,
   and our eternal home.[28]

Tune: ST. ANNE, CM, 8.6.8.6

Holy God of all creation, you will surely comfort your people. You will make their deserts like Eden, their wastelands like a garden. Joy and gladness will be found among them, thanksgiving and the sound of singing. (*Inspired by Isaiah 51:3)*

3. WILDFIRE

Fire refines, purifies, clarifies; it heats homes and hearths, cooks our food, lights up the dark night, and warms us around the campfire. Fire symbolizes passion, warmth, danger, truth, and the Holy Spirit. Fire attracts and repels; it builds up and breaks down. Wildfire is fire out of control—the deadly combination of heat, drought, and wind. All it takes is a little spark to unleash a maelstrom.

Please, O God of Hosts, come back! Look down from heaven, and watch over this vine, the root planted by your own hand, the shoot you have raised up as your own. It is now cut down and thrown into the fire, consumed by the flames. *(Psalm 80:14–16a)*[29]

PRAYERS

Help us, Lord! We need your help! Send rain now! Hold back the wind! We see people fleeing wildfires; they grab each other and go, leaving everything, not knowing if they will ever see their homes again. The smell of smoke, ash falling, the glow of flames devouring the landscape, every living creature running for dear life. We are terrified by this fiery power. Send rain now! Hold back the wind! Spare our communities; spare our land.

God our refuge, there are many who don't know where they will sleep tonight. Bless all who open their arms and their homes to help those who need sheltering. As communities face this crisis, we need your assurance for the fearful, your comfort for the bereaved, your hope for the despairing. God, help us in our time of need, in ways we can't even think about yet. And send rain now! ***Amen.*** *(Carol Penner)*[30]

3. Wildfire

Our heavenly God, Creator of all things: We call out to you in these desperate times as fires have swept across several parts of our country. Our hearts cry out to you for those who have lost loved ones, and those who have lost properties in the wake of these ravaging fires. We pray, in your mercy, restrain the forces of nature from creating catastrophic damage; in your mercy protect human life. Guard those volunteers, rural fire service personnel, and emergency services who selflessly step into the breach to fight these fires. Guide police and authorities who help evacuate and shelter those who are displaced. Bring comfort and healing to all who suffer loss. Remembering your promises of old that seedtime and harvest will never cease, we pray that you will open the heavens to send refreshing rain upon our parched land. We pray that in your miraculous power you will bring forth rain to quench these fires and to bring life back into the earth, so that crops may grow and farmers may bring forth the harvest of the land again. We bring these requests before your throne, in the name of your Son, who died and rose again. ***Amen.*** *(Glenn Davies)*[31]

CANTICLE ISAIAH 43:1–2, 5, 18–21

But now thus says the Lord,
he who created you, O Jacob,
he who formed you, O Israel:

Do not fear, for I have redeemed you;
I have called you by name; you are mine.

When you pass through the waters, I will be with you,
and through the rivers, they shall not overwhelm you;

when you walk through fire you shall not be burned,
and the flame shall not consume you. . . .

Do not fear, for I am with you;
I will bring your offspring from the east,
and from the west I will gather you . . .

Do not remember the former things
or consider the things of old.

I am about to do a new thing;
now it springs forth; do you not perceive it?

I will make a way in the wilderness
and rivers in the desert.

The wild animals will honor me,
the jackals and the ostriches,

for I give water in the wilderness,
rivers in the desert,

to give drink to my chosen people,
the people whom I formed for myself

so that they might declare my praise. (*NRSVue*)

SCRIPTURE JOEL 1:8A, 10–12, 19–20; 2:3, 10, 12–13A

Lament . . .

The fields are devastated,
the ground mourns,
for the grain is destroyed,
the wine dries up,
the oil fails.

Be dismayed, you farmers;
wail, you vinedressers,
over the wheat and the barley,
for the crops of the field are ruined.
The vine withers;
the fig tree droops.
Pomegranate, palm, and apple—
all the trees of the field are dried up;
surely, joy withers away
among the people. . . .

To you, O LORD, I cry,
for fire has devoured
the pastures of the wilderness,
and flames have burned
all the trees of the field.

Even the wild animals cry to you
    because the watercourses are dried up,
and fire has devoured
    the pastures of the wilderness. . . .

Fire devours in front of them,
    and behind them a flame burns.
Before them the land is like the garden of Eden,
    but after them a desolate wilderness,
    and nothing escapes them. . . .

The earth quakes before them;
    the heavens tremble.
The sun and the moon are darkened,
    and the stars withdraw their shining. . . .

Yet even now, says the LORD,
    return to me with all your heart,
with fasting, with weeping, and with mourning;
    rend your hearts and not your clothing.
Return to the LORD your God,
    for he is gracious and merciful,
slow to anger, abounding in steadfast love . . . (*NRSVue*)

LITANY TALITHA ARNOLD

God of all creation, of rain and fire, of ponderosa and piñon, of desert and forest, we your people lift our prayers to you,

Lord, hear our prayer.

For rain in this thirsty land and for hope in this hard time,

Lord, hear our prayer.

For all people who have lost their homes, communities and livelihoods, for indigenous people whose homeland for generations is now scorched and burned, for all persons who have been forced to evacuate or who are still in danger,

Lord, hear our prayer.

For the animals and birds who have lost their homes to fire, for your plants and trees, rivers and lakes, and all creation that is suffering because of drought and fire and often because of human greed or human carelessness,

Lord, hear our prayer.

For farmers, ranchers, and the people of rural communities whose lives and livelihoods are threatened by drought; for landscapers, business people, and day workers who may lose their jobs in this dry time,

Lord, hear our prayer.

For the just and wise use of the water you have given us, to be gracious stewards of your creation and good neighbors with all people,

Lord, hear our prayer.

For the wisdom to conserve and the grace to share the natural resources you have given all of us,

Lord, hear our prayer.

For city councils and church councils, county commissioners and tribal governments, state authorities and national leaders, to have your courage and your vision to make hard decisions for the common good,

Lord, hear our prayer.

Gracious God, you who hear every prayer of every heart, hear now the prayers of this people that we lift to you.

A time of silent prayer.

Hear all our prayers, spoken and unspoken. Remind us that you are the one who listens and who hears.

Help us to be a people who also listen and hear—to one another, to our brothers and sisters, to all creation. Give us the courage and grant us the wisdom to love one another and this earth as you do.[32]

3. *Wildfire*

REFLECTION JAMIE HOLMES

Started by a spark from a faulty power line in a nearby canyon and fueled by drought-ravaged forests and high winds, the Camp Fire burned extraordinarily hot and fast. Outdated forest management policies, droughts induced by climate change, negligent power companies, and urban encroachment into wildlands are among the causes.

The cellphone emergency-notification systems for Paradise were either nonexistent or pitiful, and only offered in English. Most of those who died didn't have time or means to escape. Some chose not to evacuate, believing the fire would be put out. Four died in their cars on their street in gridlock.

Survivors tell how they called loved ones from their cars to say last good-byes until the cell towers burned and phones became useless. Parents of children who were at school desperately hoped their youngsters would be rescued when they couldn't reach them to save them. Teachers put students in their own vehicles when the buses became full. One bus driver tore his T-shirt into strips for the children to cover their mouths to avoid breathing the grit in the air. A paraplegic patient who was home alone told me she'd managed to tape a "help" sign on a window with her kindergartner's construction paper.

As a volunteer chaplain at Enloe Medical Center, a three-hundred-bed regional hospital in nearby Chico, California, the command center called me in as the fire incinerated most of my hometown. Many have been admitted with stress-related, respiratory, or cardiac conditions. Over a year later, we still hear anguished chronicles from our patients.

Some survivors weep when telling me about their traumatic evacuation experiences and what happened to their lives, their homes, and their animals. But just as often catastrophe is recounted without any emotion at all. Post-traumatic stress syndrome is prevalent but not always obvious at first.

Even so, aid and compassion have also prevailed. One-time pop-up sites distributed everything from shovels to shoes within a few hours as word spread. Money arrived from all over the world. Governmental agencies and generous nonprofits rushed into action. Many people took strangers and their animals into their homes for days, weeks, or months.

The spiritual toll has been high. Some have survived in body but not so well in heart or spirit. But we've also seen people who made it through 2019 and the critical first anniversary of the devastation with renewed resilience.

I believe it is ultimately the sustaining power of love—both human and divine, given and received—that has enabled victims to become survivors. It is summed up in the simple but profound children's prayer said every Sunday in my church: "God, we love you. Thank you for loving us. Help us to love others."[33]

Jamie Holmes, a volunteer chaplain in nearby Chico, grew up in Paradise, California, which made international news on November 8, 2018, when it became the site of the deadliest and most destructive fire in California's history. 52,000 people fled for their lives on the only four roads off the ridge, 19,000 buildings—mostly homes—were destroyed, and eighty-six people died.

PRAYERS

Almighty God, who alone created the beauty and the bounty of our land, who lovingly cares for everyone—from the workers in the field to the owners of the field—be with your people now in the midst of the wildfires. Bring an end to the loss of lives and the loss of homes. Bring aid to the firefighters who, by serving others, serve you. Give them courage and strength to persevere, to find the ability in their bodies and souls to keep working for another day or hour or minute. Ease the winds that spread the flames and disperse the smoke that covers the sky. ***Amen.*** *(Antonio De Loera-Brust)*[34]

Be our companion and guide, O holy God, as the cities are rebuilt. May no one be left behind. May all be remembered as you remember all. As you led the Hebrew people through the desert, lead your people now. From immigrants who face unique obstacles to farmworkers who continue to labor in the fields despite dangerous smoke, to families who have lost loved ones, to those who have lost everything they have built over a lifetime; may all be included and cared for as we rebuild, guided by your Spirit. May our hearts never turn away from you or from each other. May we see you in the faces of those in need. May we see your work in the hands of all those who reach out to help. ***Amen.*** *(Antonio De Loera-Brust)*[35]

Come, Holy Spirit, enkindle in us the fire of your love; fill the hearts of your people and renew the face of the earth. Fill us with compassion and mercy to stand with our sisters and brothers affected by the fires. Give us strength to join in their suffering and bear witness to their pain. Instead of the driving winds that add fuel to the fires, come as a gentle breath. Bring fresh air to drive away the toxic fumes and ashen skies. Breathe new life into us; inspire us with love to care for one another and for the earth. Come now, Holy Spirit, and renew the face of the earth. ***Amen.*** *(Peter Bierer)*[36]

HYMN CAROLYN WINFREY GILLETTE

1. O God of mighty wind and flame who fills your church with power,
   we gather here in Jesus' name, to ask your help this hour.
   When nature's might seems far too strong and flames are swirling high,
   when days bring fear and nights are long, Lord, hear your people's cry.

2. Some, having not the time to pack, lost all they left behind;
   we pray that when they can go back, your strength is what they'll find.
   As they are grieving, bending low to sift through ash and stone,
   we pray that soon again, they'll know the comfort of a home.

3. Some labor hard with little pay; their blessings seem so few.
   They have no homes to save this day—God, keep them close to you.
   Some risk their lives and give up sleep to fight the fires so long;
   in this, the vigil that they keep, God, keep them safe and strong.

4. O God in whom we live and move—when lives are torn apart,
   give us, your church, abundant love to heal each broken heart.
   And when we see our neighbor's pain, give us the grace to share,
   till like a gentle, needed rain, new hope will fill the air.[37]

Tune: ELLACOMBE, CMD

May the presence of God the Creator give us strength; may the presence of God the redeemer give us peace; may the presence of God the sustainer give us comfort; may the presence of God the sanctifier give us love. ***Amen.*** *(United Methodist Church)*[38]

4. WILD WINDS

As worldwide temperatures rise and oceans become warmer, the atmosphere becomes more unstable, making storms stronger and more frequent. Winds blow wildly. The intensity of tornadoes, hurricanes, typhoons, and cyclones is magnified due to the changing physics and chemistry of the earth among the multiple factors contributing to climate change.

The universe unfolds in God, who fills it completely. Hence, there is a mystical meaning to be found in a leaf, in a mountain trail, in a dewdrop, in a poor person's face. The ideal is not only to pass from the exterior to the interior to discover the action of God in the soul, but also to discover God in all things. *(Pope Francis)*[39]

PRAYERS

God of power, may the boldness of your Spirit transform us, may the gentleness of your Spirit lead us, may the gifts of your Spirit be our goal and our strength always. Praise and glory to you, creator Spirit of God; you make our bread Christ's body to heal and reconcile and to make us the body of Christ. You make our wine Christ's living sacrificial blood to redeem the world. You are truth. You come like the wind of heaven, unseen, unbidden. Like the dawn you illuminate the world around us; you grant us a new beginning every day. You warm and comfort us. You give us courage and fire beyond our everyday resources. Be with us, Holy Spirit in all we say or think, in all we do this and every day. ***Amen***. *(The Church of the Province of New Zealand)*[40]

O holy God, you hear our cries and you know our needs before we ask; we intercede on behalf of everyone affected by these storms. Bless, keep, protect, and comfort each and every one of them. Meet every need. We pray for the safety of every missing person. Let every grieving family know of your love. Guide and strengthen every person helping in the search, support, treatment, and cleanup effort. We thank you, Father, Jesus Christ and the Holy Spirit, for hearing our prayers. ***Amen.*** *(St. Mary's Parish, Winnipeg, Manitoba)*[41]

PSALM 121

I lift up my eyes to the mountains—
from where will my help come?

My help comes from YHWH,
who made heaven and earth!

YHWH won't let our footsteps slip:
our Guardian never sleeps.

The guardian of Israel
will never slumber, never sleep!
YHWH is our guardian;
YHWH is our shade:

with God by our side,
the sun cannot overpower us by day,
nor the moon at night.

YHWH guards us from harm,
guards our lives.

YHWH guards our leaving
and our coming back,
now and forever.[42]

SCRIPTURE ACTS 27:13–20

When a moderate south wind began to blow, . . . they weighed anchor and began to sail past Crete, close to the shore. But soon a violent wind, called the northeaster, rushed down from Crete. Since the ship was caught and could not be turned head-on into the wind, we gave way to it and were driven. By running under the lee of a small island called Cauda we were scarcely able to get the ship's boat under control. After hoisting it up they took measures to undergird the ship; then, fearing that they would run on the Syrtis, they lowered the sea-anchor and so were driven. We were being pounded by the storm so violently that on the next day they began to throw the cargo overboard, and on the third day with their own hands they threw the ship's tackle overboard. When neither sun nor stars appeared for many days and no small tempest raged, all hope of our being saved was at last abandoned. (*NRSVue*)

LITANY THOMAS L. WEITZEL

Brothers and sisters in Christ, as we enter upon a time of vigilance and preparedness with the beginning of the annual *hurricane/tornado/typhoon/cyclone* season, let us humbly bring our prayers to God, the Lord of the wind and the rains, the Lord of good seasons and bad, the Lord of blessing and hope, that God might bless us with mighty power and protect us in our ways.

Lord God of all seasons, you bless us throughout the year.

You are the rain that refreshes the earth.

You are the light that shines upon all things.

You are the miracle of birth and growth.

You are the author of time and its seasons.

You set it all in motion for the benefit of all.

You are the Creator who blesses.

You are the guardian of all that you have created.

As we enter upon this season of vigilance, we ask that you watch over us.

Keep us alert and watchful in our days.

Protect us from all harm.

Keep us from devastation.

Deepen our faith,

That our fears may disappear in our trust in you.

Bless those public agencies responsible for storm tracking, watches, and preparedness.

Bless their plans, their practices, their skills, their dedication.

And at the time of extreme watchfulness,

Bless their concentration, and our willingness to follow their advice and commands.

The eyes of all look to you, O Lord.

You open your hand, and satisfy the desire of every living thing.

Lord of the universe and the four winds, hear our petitions and supplications. In you alone is our salvation. In you alone do we find our lives safe. As once you were the guide and protection of your people Israel in pillars of wind and fire, so also guide and protect us, your people of today, and keep us in safety and peace all our days; through our Lord Jesus Christ, to whom with you and the Holy Spirit, belong all honor and glory, now and forever. ***Amen.***[43]

REFLECTION ANTONIO LABIAO

In early November, we were hit by four typhoons in the Philippines, one after the other. I grew up in Mindanao and there were no typhoons when I was a child. Now, not only can they strike any time of the year but they're getting more and more frequent and powerful and they strike every year.

Goni (or Rolly, as it was called in the Philippines) was the most powerful typhoon to hit us. It was a category 5 super typhoon, the most powerful typhoon to hit the Philippines in twenty years. Over 350,000 people had to be evacuated from their homes and 4.8 million individuals were affected. Typhoon Vamco (Ulysses), which came afterwards, also had a massive impact, affecting almost 4 million people in Luzon.

The torrential rains, howling winds and rivers of mud have brought chaos and destruction to a number of parts of the Philippines. Floods cut off towns and villages, landslides swept away homes and infrastructure, and so many people had to seek shelter and help. . . .

The situation in the Philippines is very serious. Every year the typhoons are getting stronger and the impact is getting greater. We can't just keep scaling up our emergency response every year as these weather events damage more and more lives. We need to address the real cause of these calamities—climate change, the degradation of our mountains, illegal logging, quarrying, and unsustainable farming practices. This is not just the work of government, but of the church and of everyone. . . .

Our vision must reach beyond emergency response. When we talk about preventing climate change, we can't just do this alone in the Philippines, we need the help of the global community. It's only by working together that we make sure future generations are safe.[44]

Antonio Labiao, a Catholic priest, is executive director of Caritas Philippines, a branch of a Catholic aid organization that works in most countries of the world at the grassroots level to reach out to the poor and vulnerable with love and help in rebuilding their lives and communities after catastrophes, such as the devastating typhoons in the Philippines.

PRAYERS

God of the universe, at the dawn of creation your Spirit breathed on the waters, making them the wellspring of all holiness. You created the oceans and rivers, and all that dwell within them, and at your word the wind and the waves were born. The seasons follow your plan, and the tides rise and fall on your command. In both calm and storm, you are with us. On the Sea of Galilee, even when the disciples began to fear, Jesus showed that he was Lord over the waters by rebuking the storms, so that all would know that even the wind and the waves obey him. Creator God, we ask you to calm the wind and the waves of the approaching hurricane *(or tornado)*, and spare those in its path from harm. Help those who are in its way to reach safety. Open our hearts in generosity to all who need help in the coming days. In all things and in all times, help us to remember that even when life seems dark and stormy, you are in the boat with us, guiding us to safety. ***Amen.*** *(James Martin, SJ)*[45]

Merciful Counselor, we grieve with communities suffering from disasters and struggling to recover. Speed the restoration of community life so children can feel secure again. Give families strength and perseverance while they rebuild their homes and livelihoods. We pray for disaster survivors that they may find refuge in you. ***Amen.*** *(Heather Klinger)*[46]

HYMN ADAM M. L. TICE

1. In floods of chaos, seas of grief,
loud rushing wind and pounding waves,
will waters drown our sure belief
that, in disaster, Jesus saves?

2. When with one voice the people cry,
but no one hears the poor and meek,
can we believe—as children die—
that God is strong when we are weak?

3. If in the comfort of our ease
we sit and watch the chaos grow,
ignoring desperate cries and pleas,
who is this God we claim to know?

4. Where charity and love are found,
there God will always be.
Love such as this cannot be drowned
by any storm or crashing sea.[47]

Tunes: WINCHESTER NEW or WAREHAM, LM, 8.8.8.8

Now may the God of peace give us peace at all times in all ways. May our Lord Jesus Christ give us everlasting encouragement and good hope and strengthen us in every way. *(Inspired by 2 Thessalonians 3:16)*

5. FLOOD

Flooding is natural and to be expected every spring. Flooding waters carry nutrients that replenish soil; they carry out wastes; they renew wetlands and recharge underground aquifers. Flooding may become disastrous when the direction of rivers is altered to suit human desires, when building occurs on floodplains, and at times of excessive rain or snowmelt.

YHWH is good, a stronghold in a day of troubles, protecting those who take refuge in God, even in a rushing flood. *(Nahum:1:7)*[48]

PRAYERS

Blessed are you, sacred Source of all life. Blessed are you who has made the entire universe your holy temple. Sacred are the mountains and valleys, prairies and fields of this planet. Holy are the forests and meadows, the canyons and oceans deep, the cities and villages—all sacred space. All who dwell upon this planet walk on holy ground; all are stewards of your earthly shrine. Now, sacred Source of life, we pray for the special needs of earth (: __________). ***Amen.*** *(Edward Hays)*[49]

Faithful and loving God, we pray for our sisters and brothers affected by the intense rains (in __________). Rescue all who are marooned by flood waters. Shelter those who have had to leave home. Comfort the distressed; hold the bereaved. Cause the rains to cease and the waters to subside. Support those who are working to respond. Grant them all the support they need to reach the most vulnerable and those at great risk. Provide for all their essential needs by the generosity and concern of your people from around the world who long for your will to be done on earth as in heaven. In the name of your beloved Son we pray, ***Amen.*** *(Christian Aid, UK)*[50]

PSALM 29:3–11

The voice of the LORD is over the waters;
the God of glory thunders;
the LORD on the immensity of waters.

The voice of the LORD is full of power;
the voice of the LORD is full of splendor.

The voice of the LORD shatters cedars;
the LORD shatters the cedars of Lebanon,

making Lebanon leap like a calf,
and Sirion like a young wild ox.

The voice of the LORD flashes flames of fire.

The voice of the LORD shakes the wilderness;
the LORD shakes the wilderness of Kadesh.

The voice of the LORD rends the oak tree
and strips the forest bare.

In God's temple all cry, "Glory!"

The LORD sits enthroned above the flood;
the LORD sits as king forever.

Give strength to your people, O LORD.

O LORD, bless your people with peace.[51]

SCRIPTURE GENESIS 7:1A, 11–16A, 17–24

Then the LORD said to Noah, "Go into the ark, you and all your household. . . ."

In the six hundredth year of Noah's life, in the second month, on the seventeenth day of the month, on that day all the fountains of the great deep burst forth, and the windows of the heavens were opened. The rain fell on the earth for forty days and forty nights. On the very same day Noah with his sons, Shem and Ham and Japheth, and Noah's wife and the three wives of his sons entered the ark, they and every wild animal of every kind and all domestic animals of every kind and every creeping thing that creeps on the earth and every bird of every kind. They went into the ark with Noah, two and two of all flesh in which there was the breath of life. And those that entered, male and female of all flesh, went in as God had commanded him. . . .

The flood continued forty days on the earth, and the waters increased and bore up the ark, and it rose high above the earth. The waters swelled and increased greatly on the earth, and the ark floated on the face of the waters. The waters swelled so mightily on the earth that all the high mountains under the whole heaven were covered; the waters swelled above the mountains, covering them fifteen cubits deep. And all flesh died that moved on the earth, birds, domestic animals, wild animals, all swarming creatures that swarm on the earth, and all human beings; everything on dry land in whose nostrils was the breath of life died. He blotted out every living thing that was on the face of the ground, human beings and animals and creeping things and birds of the air; they were blotted out from the earth. Only Noah was left and those that were with him in the ark. And the waters swelled on the earth for one hundred fifty days. (*NRSVue*)

LITANY JOHN G. HAMILTON

Lord, all around us the waters are rising.

We feel so helpless, for we cannot stop the rain from falling or the waters from rising.

We feel so powerless, for the current is strong and our bodies are tired.

We feel so empty, for our possessions are floating away or anchored in the muddy water.

Lord, all around us the waters are rising.

Grant us your strength, since ours is somewhere downstream.

Grant us your patience, since ours is drowning.

Grant us your perspective, since our loss is in replaceable things, not irreplaceable grace.

Give us eyes to see how precious your gifts are: family and friends, faith and mercy.

And Lord, when the waters rise around us and our spirits, and our faith and hope are swept downstream, help us to remember how you got us through this flood.

In your Son's name. ***Amen.***[52]

REFLECTION JENNIFER OLADIPO

The Cajundome—it was a mega-shelter, a mini-city full of people who had fled Hurricane Katrina and had nowhere else to go. . . .

Evacuees make homes, like hundreds of bees in a hive, as best they can on and around these six-by-four-foot cots. . . . If you were an evacuee you'd pick up your blanket bundle and toiletries. . . . Over there is the communications center, the makeshift kiosk where you could make a phone call or leave a note on the message board so any of the three thousand or more other residents can read it. Maybe one of them has seen your cousin. Maybe one of them *is* your cousin. . . .

Given the large number of people here, the place seems oddly quiet. . . . Sometimes you hear a scream, and turn to see someone collapsing in tears by the telephone. You come to know this means that somebody didn't make it through the floods.

Watch seasons change inside this city, overlapping cycles that mark the passing time and link this little world to the larger one beyond. . . . As water recedes from city streets a hundred miles away so too is the shelter drained of evacuees. . . . You think the worst is over, the lesson learned. You trust that this has been the final rallying call, that this mini-city will return forever to the business of basketball and corporate conventions. But you will see, years later, that you were probably wrong.[53]

The writer, Jennifer Oladipo, volunteered as a trash collector with the Red Cross in an evacuation convention and sports center in Lafayette, Louisiana, following Hurricane Katrina in August, 2005. The storm slammed coastal Louisiana and Mississippi, collapsing levees and flooding the vulnerable low lands. One thousand eight hundred people lost their lives; thousands found refuge in shelters such as the Cajundome, described here.

PRAYERS

God of our life, whose presence sustains us in every circumstance, in the aftermath of storm and distress, we welcome the restoring power of your love and compassion.

We open our hearts in sorrow, gratitude, and hope: that those who have been spared nature's fury as well as those whose lives are changed forever by ravages of water may find solace, sustenance, and strength in the days of recovery and restoration to come.

We open ourselves to the stories of those communities and individuals deeply affected, and pray in grief, remembering the lives that have been lost as floodwaters raged. We lift our voices in sorrow and compassion for families who have lost loved ones, homes, or livelihoods.

We ask for sustaining courage for those who are suffering; for wisdom and diligence among those assessing damage and directing relief efforts; and for generosity to flow as powerfully as rivers and streams, as we, your people, respond to the deep human needs beginning to emerge in the wake of the storm.

In these days of relief, assessment, and response, open our eyes, our hearts, and our hands to the needs of your children and to the movements of your Spirit, who flows in us like the river whose streams make glad the city of God, and the hearts of all who dwell in it and in you. In the name of Christ the healer, we pray. ***Amen.*** *(Laurie Kraus)*[54]

Great and merciful God, your life is the source of the whole world's life; your mercy is our only hope; your eyes watch over all your creatures; you know the secrets of our hearts. By your life-giving Spirit, draw us into your presence, with lives moved by your love, through him who has led us to your heart of love, Jesus Christ our Lord. ***Amen.*** *(Church of South India)*[55]

HYMN CAROLYN WINFREY GILLETTE

1. When waters roar and foam and overtake the land,
when homes along the shore are filled with mud or sand,
when mighty storm winds blow and bring us to our knees;
Creator God, renew our faith in times like these.

2. When neighborhoods we love are lost in just a day,
when homes and lives and livelihoods are swept away,

when all that we have left are precious memories;
O Christ, give healing, strength, and hope in times like these.

3. When help is hard to find, when others need a hand,
when people suffer, tired and cold, throughout the land,
may we your church respond to struggling neighbors' needs;
O Spirit, teach us how to love in times like these.[56]

Tune: LEONI, 6.6.8.4.D

May the strength of God pilot us. May the power of God preserve us. May the wisdom of God instruct us. May the hand of God protect us. May the way of God direct us. May the shield of God defend us. May the host of God guard us against the snares of evil and the temptations of the world. May Christ be with us, Christ before us, Christ over us. May our salvation, O God, be always ours this day and forevermore. ***Amen***. *(Attributed to St. Patrick)*[57]

6. EARTHQUAKE

When earth shakes under our feet and buildings topple, we ask the cosmic questions: "God, where are you?" "Are you in the eye of the storm and the earthquake?" "Are you with us in our suffering?" When the rattling stops, we may respond like Job, "[We] know that you can do all things and that no purpose of yours can be thwarted." (Job 42:2 NRSVue)

Cast your burden on God who will sustain you. (*Psalm 55:22*)[58]

PRAYERS

Most merciful and compassionate God, giver of life and love, hear our prayers and let our cries come unto you. We weep with your people. We hear the cries of orphaned children and laments of bereaved parents. We feel the desperation of those searching for loved ones. We behold the silence of vanished villages. We see the devastation. We are overwhelmed by the enormity of it all. Our hearts are hushed; our minds are numb. Let not our hands be stopped, our voices dumb. God of the universe, open our hearts to feel your compassion. Galvanize in us the act of continued giving. Bond us to our sisters and brothers in need. Comfort and heal the injured, the bereaved, the lost. Strengthen the aid workers and medical personnel. Bolster the resolve of governments and those with power to help. Open through this tragedy pathways to partnerships and peace. In your name of mercy and healing and compassion we pray. ***Amen.*** *(Wilma T. Jakobsen)*[59]

We mourn the death and destruction (in __________), O Lord, and we pray for those who have died. May their souls rest in peace; may their families be comforted. We pray for the living survivors: be with them, Lord, in this traumatic time. May they experience your healing, in their spirits as well as in their bodies. We pray for the communities affected: may they come together in solidarity to rebuild and to affirm new life amid the ancient stones. ***Amen.*** *(St. Mary's Parish, Winnipeg, Manitoba)*[60]

PSALM 60:2–5, 9–12

You have caused the land to quake; you have torn it open;
  repair the cracks in it, for it is tottering.

You have made your people suffer hard things;
  you have given us wine to drink that made us reel.

You have set up a banner for those who fear you,
  to rally to it out of bowshot. . . .

Give victory with your right hand and answer us,
  so that those whom you love may be rescued. . . .

Who will bring me to the fortified city?
  Who will lead me to Edom?

Have you not rejected us, O God?
  You do not go out, O God, with our armies.

O grant us help against the foe,
  for human help is worthless.

With God we shall do valiantly;
  it is he who will tread down our foes. (*NRSVue*)

SCRIPTURE ZECHARIAH 14:4–9, 11

On that day his feet shall stand on the Mount of Olives, which lies before Jerusalem on the east; and the Mount of Olives shall be split in two from east to west by a very wide valley, so that one half of the mount shall withdraw northward and the other half southward. And you shall flee by the valley of the LORD's mountain, for the valley between the mountains shall reach to Azal, and you shall flee as you fled from the earthquake in the days of

King Uzziah of Judah. Then the Lord my God will come and all the holy ones with him.

On that day there shall not be either cold or frost. And there shall be continuous day (it is known to the Lord), not day and not night, for at evening time there shall be light.

On that day living waters shall flow out from Jerusalem, half of it to the eastern sea and half of it to the western sea; it shall continue in summer as in winter.

And the Lord will become king over all the earth; on that day the Lord will be one and his name one. . . .

And it shall be inhabited, for never again shall it be doomed to destruction; Jerusalem shall abide in security. (*NRSVue*)

LITANY MELISSA BILLS AND ANNE EDISON-ALBRIGHT

God our refuge, we lift up our prayers with all who are suffering because of this earthquake. Bring an end to poverty, climate change, colonialism, and all forces that make natural disasters more profound. Empower advocates of your justice and healing, and hold in your love all who are grieving this day. Lamb of God, be with us now,

Give us your peace, we pray.

God is our refuge and strength, a very present help in trouble.

Therefore we will not fear, though the earth should change, though the mountains shake in the heart of the sea;

though its waters roar and foam, though the mountains tremble with its tumult.

The Lord of hosts is with us; the God of Jacob is our refuge.

God has not forgotten us. God mourns with us for all that we've lost.

God hears our cries; God hears the cries of the world.

Injustice and tyranny compound disaster. We rage against powers that deal poverty and death.

The Lord of hosts is with us; the God of Jacob is our refuge.

Listen! The people whose world shakes are speaking. God is speaking through all who are broken.

God walks with us; what can we fear? Afraid and brave, we walk together.

God is our refuge and strength,

The Lord of hosts is with us; the God of Jacob is our refuge.[61]

REFLECTION NICHOLAS ROXBURGH

The building in Kathmandu around me began to sway as I sat at my desk working. At first it was gentle, but then it grew more violent. . . . Dust and plaster from the ceiling began to fall around me as the quake continued. Fearing the building would collapse I made the decision to move. . . . I made my way through dust and debris to the front door and out onto the street. Initially there was an eerie calm before people began to cautiously emerge, dust filling the streets.

Just a few doors down . . . a hospital stood . . . , its staff out on the street fearing collapse. Within minutes injured people began to arrive, in cars, taxis, on foot, being carried by others. It was immediately clear there had been casualties. The lifeless bodies of two young children were carried in, while countless others arrived with a variety of horrific injuries—many having been hurt by falling masonry, others having been pulled from collapsed buildings. . . .

As night fell, many crowded into the few areas of open space in Kathmandu, using tarpaulins as a temporary shelter against the elements. As dawn broke on Sunday, the aftershocks continued to rock the city, each one sending people running for cover.

During the day it began to rain, leaving those who have been left homeless—or too fearful to return to their homes—exposed in the cold, wet weather.

People have spent the day working together to find survivors in collapsed buildings, sharing water and food where they can, and forming temporary shelters. . . . The immediate need is clear—shelter, food, and water, along with support that will help rebuild this beautiful country.[62]

Nicholas Roxburgh had been working in Nepal for nine months on a rural water system management project when the devastating earthquake of April

2015 struck. Entire villages were buried and thousands became homeless. Twenty-two thousand people were injured and nine thousand killed, including twenty-two climbers who were killed in an earthquake-triggered avalanche on Mount Everest.

PRAYERS

God, our refuge and strength, we pray with and for the people who are suffering in the aftermath of the earthquake. Bless the memory of all who died in this disaster (*especially* ___________), and bind our hearts together with all who grieve and rebuild. Draw near to all communities and nations who have suffered natural disasters in recent memory (*other natural disasters may be named*). Support relief workers and international aid organizations as they generously offer themselves in time of need. Mitigate the effects of future disasters by empowering us to work for economic justice, to seek the care of creation, and to listen faithfully to the voices of our siblings across the globe. Bring hope to our hearts by your promise to make among us a new creation, where all nature is again at peace. Into your hands we commend ourselves, our world, and all for whom we pray, in the name of Christ and by the power of the Holy Spirit. ***Amen.*** *(Melissa Bills and Anne Edison-Albright)*[63]

Holy One, you are our comfort and strength in times of sudden disaster, crisis, or chaos. Surround us now with your grace and peace through storm or earthquake, fire or flood. By your Spirit, lift up those who have fallen, sustain those who work to rescue or rebuild, and fill us with the hope of your new creation; through Jesus Christ, our rock and redeemer. ***Amen.*** *(Presbyterian Church USA)*[64]

HYMN ANDREW PRATT

1. Tectonic plates beneath the ocean's surface,
uplifted, twisting life and limb and wave.
The landscape that was home has lost its features,
destruction means that few are left to save.

2. An empty chair amid such devastation
where cars, like toys, are lifted, spun about;

and here we wait and pray in helpless anguish;
and "Where is God" we want to cry and shout.

3. Incarnate God, we need your present Spirit
to live within your people at this time,
to energize our prayerful words and actions,
to offer grace to life's discordant rhyme.

4. God, offer hope to those who feel forsaken,
to those whose lives have spun and turned around;
to those whose grief defies all consolation,
bring grace and love and hope and solid ground.[65]

Tune: INTERCESSOR, 11.10.11.10. Words © 2011
Stainer & Bell, Ltd. (admin. Hope Publishing)

Let nothing disturb you. Let nothing frighten you. All things pass. God does not change. (*Attributed to St. Teresa of Avila)*[66]

7. TSUNAMI

Few of us will forget images of the hundred-foot waves that suddenly hit Sumatra Island in Indonesia on Christmas and Boxing Day 2004, or the sight of screaming children running for safety. The tsunami was caused by a massive underwater earthquake that ruptured the fault lines where the Indian and Australian tectonic plates meet. One hundred and seventy thousand people were killed immediately in Banda Aceh, and one hundred thousand more in the following days as tsunami waves rolled over coastlines in India, Thailand, Sri Lanka, and as far distant as South Africa.

God really does lie hidden and unknown beneath every person in need. God pleads for compassion and liberation. God wants to be helped. It is important to know this. Even more important and decisive is offering help, stooping down and taking the other person's cross on our shoulders, and walking together. *(Leonardo Boff)*[67]

PRAYERS

Dear God and Savior of all, we are crushed in spirit and filled with grief and uncertainty in the wake of the tsunami. Looking over the ravaged land and shore, we ask where you are. Are you there in the pounding waves that demolished the coastline? Are you there in the devastation and rubble, the collapsed and waterlogged homes, schools, and businesses? Are you there as the angry sea devours the people, washing away their lives and hopes and dreams? Are you there in the sobbing child clinging to the swaying branch, crying for mother? Are you there in the broken-hearted who have lost their dear ones?

Yes! Hard as it is, we still say, "Yes." Yes, we believe you hold and keep us in these worst of circumstances. Just as you were there as the crucified Jesus died on the cross, be with your crucified people as they rebuild their lives and communities in the true knowledge that you are with us always, even to the end of time. ***Amen.*** *(Anne Rowthorn)*[68]

Holy God, source of life, lover of souls, out of the depths we call to you; in the face of incomprehensible anguish and sorrow, we lift the cries of our distress and implore you to show mercy upon those who are suffering from the destruction of (*this storm surge*). We pray for those who have died and for their loved ones who grieve, asking you to hold them in the arms of your love; we pray for those who have been injured in body, mind, or spirit and ask you to heal them; we pray for those who are homeless and wandering, for families torn asunder and ask you to shelter them. Strengthen the hands and hearts of those who assist in relief efforts and grant us all firm resolve to stand with our neighbors who are in need, to love them and to offer our generous support of them in this their time of trouble; through Jesus Christ our Lord, who lives and reigns with you and the Holy Spirit, now and forever. ***Amen.*** *(William Stokes)*[69]

PSALM 107:23–30

Some went down to the sea in ships,
    doing business on the mighty waters;

they saw the deeds of the LORD,
    his wondrous works in the deep.

For he commanded and raised the stormy wind,
    which lifted up the waves of the sea.

They mounted up to heaven; they went down to the depths;
    their courage melted away in their calamity;

they reeled and staggered like drunkards
    and were at their wits' end.

Then they cried to the LORD in their trouble,
    and he brought them out from their distress;

he made the storm be still,
   and the waves of the sea were hushed.

Then they were glad because they had quiet,
   and he brought them to their desired haven. (*NRSVue*)

SCRIPTURE ROMANS 8:18–25, 35–39

I consider that the sufferings of this present time are not worth comparing with the glory about to be revealed to us. For the creation waits with eager longing for the revealing of the children of God, for the creation was subjected to futility, not of its own will, but by the will of the one who subjected it, in hope that the creation itself will be set free from its enslavement to decay and will obtain the freedom of the glory of the children of God. We know that the whole creation has been groaning together as it suffers together the pains of labor, and not only the creation, but we ourselves, who have the first fruits of the Spirit, groan inwardly while we wait for adoption, the redemption of our bodies. For in hope we were saved. Now hope that is seen is not hope, for who hopes for what one already sees? But if we hope for what we do not see, we wait for it with patience. . . .

Who will separate us from the love of Christ? Will affliction or distress or persecution or famine or nakedness or peril or sword? As it is written,

"For your sake we are being killed all day long;
   we are accounted as sheep to be slaughtered."

No, in all these things we are more than victorious through him who loved us. For I am convinced that neither death, nor life, nor angels, nor rulers, nor things present, nor things to come, nor powers, nor height, nor depth, nor anything else in all creation will be able to separate us from the love of God in Christ Jesus our Lord. (*NRSVue*)

LITANY CHRISTIAN AID, UNITED KINGDOM

We tremble as the earth reels and rocks, as mountains shake at their base and storm surges pound the coastline. O holy God, you are our rock, our fortress, our savior, our shield, our saving strength and our stronghold.

In our anguish, hear our prayer.

Guide rescue workers to victims who may still be alive.

In our anguish, hear our prayer.

Reunite children with their family members.

In our anguish, hear our prayer.

Wipe away every tear, and comfort those who have lost loved ones.

In our anguish, hear our prayer.

Calm those who are panicking.

In our anguish, hear our prayer.

Surround with safety and assurance all who are traumatized.

In our anguish, hear our prayer.

Shelter those who are suddenly homeless.

In our anguish, hear our prayer.

Provide food and water for victims and relief workers.

In our anguish, hear our prayer.

Be a beacon of wisdom and guidance for those directing rescue operations.

In our anguish, hear our prayer.

As you entered into the blood, sweat, and tears of life, help us to enter into lament, love, and solidarity with our sisters and brothers (in ___________).

In our anguish, hear our prayer.

Let us stand together with those you love in their time of deepest need.

God of all hope, fill our hearts with hope that they may know that you suffer with us and that we are not alone. This we pray in Jesus' name. *Amen.*[70]

REFLECTION ALMEDA M. WRIGHT

Hope is not a mere projection of good ideas into the future or simply a wish for a good outcome. Hope is an active orientation toward the good. It's connected to personal agency, the ability to act and affect the future in a positive way.

Nevertheless, hope is not tied solely to my ability to act. There's a theological dimension. Hope says God is present—God who cares about the earth and cares about us and accompanies us in the midst of suffering. Hope reminds me to look beyond the current situation to a sustaining force that is much bigger. . . . A huge narrative is at work—the sovereignty of God—which says there was a time when we were low and God provided, and there was another time when we were low and God provided. And there is this time, and there will be other times. God and God's concern for us are bigger than any [crisis]. But we still have a creative role to play—part of that is to trust God and find better solutions every day.[71]

Almeda M. Wright is associate professor of religious education at Yale Divinity School. Her research deals with African American religion, Womanist spirituality, and African American adolescent religion. In this interview with Yale Divinity School's magazine Reflections, *she spoke about hope in the midst of the pandemic.*

PRAYERS

Ruler of Creation, have mercy on all those who are suffering from the raging waters and the storming waves. Have compassion on your creatures. Look, O Lord, and see their distress; listen, God, and hear their cries. Strengthen the hands of those who bring relief; comfort the mourners; heal the wounded. Grant us wisdom and discernment to know our obligations, and open our hearts so that we may extend our hands to the devastated. Bless us so that we may walk in your ways and be your loving caress to all in need. Grant us the will and the wisdom to prevent further disaster and death. Prevent plague from descending upon your earth, and fulfill your words, "Never again shall there be another flood to destroy the earth." ***Amen. So may it be your will.*** *(Shai Held)*[72]

7. Tsunami

Living God, our refuge and strength, even the wind and sea obey your voice. Put the wind back in its place, and say to the sea: "Peace! Be still!" Fill us with great faith and save us from the surging water, so that we may tell the good news of your saving love; through Jesus Christ, our hope in the storm. ***Amen.*** *(David Gambrell)*[73]

HYMN NORMAN E. BROOKES

1. When earth's wild hidden forces
roar and shake and tilt the ground,
making fissures, cracks, and sinkholes,
in this land that once seemed sound,
then we know a power beyond us,
part of mystery profound,
part of mystery profound.

2. When earth's wild hidden forces,
crush and maim, and kill life's dreams,
taking from us those who loved us,
people long esteemed,
then we know a power beyond us,
greater than we ever dreamed,
greater than we ever dreamed.

3. When earth's wild hidden forces,
strike our cities thought secure,
damage buildings long enduring,
till, unsafe, they stand no more,
then we know a power beyond us,
sprung forth from creation's store,
sprung forth from creation's store.

4. Now let earth's wild hidden forces,
show us values long ignored
in our search for passing pleasures:
life and love, and faith in God,
in the testing and the turmoil
may God's healing power be found,
may God's healing love abound.[74]

Tune: CWM RHONDDA, 87.87.87.7

Thank you, Lord. You are the light that never goes out. You are the eye that never closes. You are the ear that is never shut. You are the mind that never gives up. You are the heart that never grows cold. You are the hand that never stops reaching. Thank you, Lord, and let us be receptive to you. ***Amen***. *(Roland J. Allen and Linda McKiernan-Allen)*[75]

8. RISING SEAS

Every country with a coastline is already being affected by rising sea levels. Those familiar with Venice, Bangkok, or Miami have seen it. Some island nations on low-lying coral atolls like Kiribati and the Marshall Islands could be completely under water in fifty years. Tuvalu and the Maldives are not far behind. Rising sea levels have already forced thousands of people to relocate to higher ground in distant lands.

Be strong and courageous; do not be frightened or dismayed, for the LORD your God is with you wherever you go. (*Joshua 1:9b NRSVue*)

PRAYERS

Lord God, maker of all worlds, we praise and adore you: thank you for our beautiful planet moving in space; thank you for light and warmth and food and life in all its forms; thank you for magnificent rainbows and night skies patterned with stars; thank you for a glimpse of your majestic universe; thank you for humankind, and for creating each one of us in your image; thank you for Jesus whose name is over all. ***Amen***. (*Michael Perry, Patrick Goodland, and Angela Griffiths*)[76]

May you raise your healing hands over all who are experiencing climate change in their countries. Please comfort those who are moving from their homelands because the sea levels are rising. Wherever they go, we pray that they may be welcomed. May they be guided to new homes where they will be able to make a living to support their families. Lord, we also pray that they will hold on to their traditions, languages, and cultures so they can live on in their future generations. ***Amen.*** (*Christina Bechara*)[77]

Lord, may those suffering from the effects of recent natural disasters ultimately put their hope in you. When the storms rage and waters rise, equip aid workers to meet the most urgent needs. In your name, dear Jesus, we pray. ***Amen.*** *(Chris Huber)*[78]

PSALM 77:1A, 14–20

I cry aloud to God,
 aloud to God. . . .

You are the God who works wonders;
 you have displayed your might among the peoples.

With your strong arm you redeemed your people,
 the descendants of Jacob and Joseph. . . .

When the waters saw you, O God,
 when the waters saw you, they were afraid;
 the very deep trembled.

The clouds poured out water;
 the skies thundered;
 your arrows flashed on every side.

The crash of your thunder was in the whirlwind;
 your lightnings lit up the world;
 the earth trembled and shook.

Your way was through the sea,
 your path through the mighty waters;
 yet your footprints were unseen.

You led your people like a flock
 by the hand of Moses and Aaron. (*NRSVue*)

8. Rising Seas

SCRIPTURE GENESIS 8:1–5, 13–22

But God remembered Noah and all the wild animals and all the domestic animals that were with him in the ark. And God made a wind blow over the earth, and the waters subsided; the fountains of the deep and the windows of the heavens were closed, the rain from the heavens was restrained, and the waters gradually receded from the earth. At the end of one hundred fifty days the waters had abated, and in the seventh month, on the seventeenth day of the month, the ark came to rest on the mountains of Ararat. The waters continued to abate until the tenth month; in the tenth month, on the first day of the month, the tops of the mountains appeared. . . .

In the six hundred first year, in the first month, on the first day of the month, the waters were dried up from the earth, and Noah removed the covering of the ark and looked and saw that the face of the ground was drying. In the second month, on the twenty-seventh day of the month, the earth was dry. Then God said to Noah, "Go out of the ark, you and your wife, and your sons and your sons' wives with you. Bring out with you every living thing that is with you of all flesh—birds and animals and every creeping thing that creeps on the earth—so that they may abound on the earth and be fruitful and multiply on the earth." So Noah went out with his sons and his wife and his sons' wives. And every animal, every creeping thing, and every bird, everything that moves on the earth, went out of the ark by families.

Then Noah built an altar to the LORD and took of every clean animal and of every clean bird and offered burnt offerings on the altar. And when the LORD smelt the pleasing odor, the LORD said in his heart, "I will never again curse the ground because of humans, for the inclination of the human heart is evil from youth; nor will I ever again destroy every living creature as I have done.

As long as the earth endures,
 seedtime and harvest, cold and heat,
summer and winter, day and night,
 shall not cease." (*NRSVue*)

LITANY ANNE ROWTHORN

O holy God of rolling seas, God in the tempest and the wave, God of scattered islands and atolls and craggy coastlands, hear the cries of your people who struggle to survive as rising seas threaten our fragile lands:

Hear us, O holy God, as the seas threaten to take our precious lands.

For all whose aquifers and wells are compromised by rising sea levels:

O holy God, hear us.

For those whose gardens and crops are laid waste by the salty seas:

O holy God, hear us.

For those losing their homes and livelihoods to the unruly tides:

O holy God, hear us.

For solidarity with each other as we address our common concerns:

O holy God, hear us.

As we contemplate leaving our familiar islands and coastlands and the graves of our ancestors:

O holy God, hear us.

As we cry out in the night wondering where we will go and how we will begin our lives anew in a foreign land:

O holy God, hear us.

We pray that nations with higher lands will receive us and give us asylum:

O holy God, hear us.

We pray that the world community will hear our cries and welcome us and our children to new and safer homes:

O holy God, hear us.

Give us courage to face unknown challenges that lie ahead, and give us new hearts and minds to welcome the new day with joy and hope:

O holy God, hear us and send us your help.[79]

REFLECTION BEN NAMAKIN

Kiribati is not just a geographical location, but a way of life. The culture is alive with vibrant traditional dances and mouthwatering local cuisine that will leave you feeling embraced by the warmth and hospitality of the locals. It's a unique experience that cannot be replicated anywhere else in the world.

Despite facing many environmental challenges, such as rising sea levels, coral bleaching, increased amount of solid waste, and overfishing, we I-Kiribati natives refuse to give up on our land. We know that by working together, we can overcome these issues and ensure a brighter future for generations to come.

As proud inheritors of our land and rich cultural heritage, we take our responsibility to preserve and protect it very seriously. It's a duty that we approach with reverence and respect for our ancestors who have passed this land and traditions down to us.

To anyone who doubts the potential of Kiribati, I invite you to come and see for yourself. Let the crystal-clear waters and gentle ocean breezes wash away your doubts, and immerse yourself in the welcoming spirit of this remarkable place. Kiribati, you hold a special place in my heart. . . .[80]

Ben Namakin and his family live in the Pacific island nation of Kiribati. He is fiercely loyal, yet he acknowledges that his atoll is deeply affected by the ravages of climate change. Already, rising sea levels are breaking sea walls, compromising drinking water, washing away homes, and killing crops. The United Nations Intergovernmental Panel on Climate Change has warned that Kiribati and five other Pacific Island nations are in danger of becoming uninhabitable by 2050. The World Bank has said that rising seas could force 140 million people to leave their homes in South Asia, sub-Saharan Africa, and Latin America.

PRAYERS

God of islands and atolls, God of rocky coastlands and sand-swept shores, God of the rolling wave and ocean depths: for millennia you have fed your island people with the richness of your bounty; their hearts beat to the rhythm of your waves; they mark the hours of their days by flow of your tides. When the heavens rumble and storms pound their coastlines, they take shelter; when sun returns and the sea calms, they are surrounded once again by unspeakable beauty.

But the oceans upon which they have depended are now troubled. Rising tides breach sea walls and contaminate wells, homes are washed away and crops are poisoned. Islanders are losing heart for they know they must move. We pray that you will rescue them just as you rescued Noah when floods overtook his land. Just as Jesus calmed the waters and led his disciples to the place where fish were plentiful, we pray that you will lead evacuating island people to life and food and fellowship where all abound. We pray that you will bless us all, sisters and brothers together, around the great cosmic altar of life. ***Amen.*** *(Anne and Jeffery Rowthorn)*[81]

We have come from far away in order to arrive at a remote destination. We have left the ravine of death in order to arrive at the top of the mountain of life. When we get to our destination we will organize ourselves. We want to get there. We can get there. We will get there in the name of Jesus who has helped us come all that great distance to arrive at our rightful destination. ***Amen***. *(Jean-Bertrand Aristide)*[82]

HYMN WILLIAM WHITING

1. Eternal Father, strong to save,
whose arm does bind the restless wave,
who bids the mighty ocean deep
its own appointed limits keep;
O hear us when we cry to thee
for those in peril from the sea.

2. O Savior, whose almighty word
the winds and waves submissive heard,
who walked upon the foaming deep,
and calm amid the rage did sleep;
O hear us when we cry to thee
for those in peril from the sea.

3. O Holy Spirit, who did brood
upon the waters dark and rude,
and bade their angry tumult cease,
and gave for wild confusion, peace;

O hear us when we cry to thee
for those in peril from the sea.

4. O Trinity of love and pow'r,
your children shield in danger's hour;
from rock and tempest, fire, and foe,
protect them where-so-e'er they go;
thus evermore shall rise to thee
glad hymns of praise from land and sea.[83]

TUNE: MELITA, 8.8.8.8.8.8

Nothing can separate us from the love of God. Wherever we go, or whatever we do, or whatever befalls us, the Eternal God is our refuge, and underneath are God's everlasting arms. *(Stephen W. Burgess and James D. Righter)*[84]

9. BLIZZARD

"The season's . . . icy fang / And churlish chiding of the winter's wind . . . bites and blows upon my body, / Even till I shrink with cold. . . ."[85] *William Shakespeare didn't know when he wrote this dialogue in* As You Like It *that he was describing a blizzard. A snowstorm becomes a blizzard when wind and snow blow at more than thirty-five miles per hour for more than three hours and reduce visibility to a quarter of a mile or less. The term* blizzard *was popularized in the United States following the harsh winters of the late 1800s.*

Praise YHWH from the earth . . . lightning and hail, snow and mist, and storms and winds that fulfill God's word. (*Psalm 148:7b, 8a*)[86]

PRAYERS

God, our Creator, as we face the storms of this world, we celebrate the wonders of the wind and the weather. Help us to see your presence, not only in the forces of nature, but also among those who suffer from natural disasters. Teach us to recognize that your wisdom is imbedded in all natural forces, a wisdom that guides, controls, and limits them. In the name of Christ, who is the Wisdom of God renewing all things in creation. ***Amen.*** *(Season of Creation)*[87]

O holy God of snow and rain, of wind and fire: at your command you stilled the turbulent waters so that the Israelites could pass through the Red Sea to the promised land. We implore you now to come among us to quell the driving snow that is covering the land. Protect all who are out on the roads—emergency medical workers, snowplow crews, law enforcement officers, long-distance truck drivers, and workers struggling to reach home. We pray for all who are homeless and lacking heat, for the elderly that they may be protected from black ice, and for all who are caught in the storm unprepared. Remember also cattle in the fields cut off from food and water and all wildlife stressed by the snow. As you parted the waters of the Red Sea, we ask you to make a path for all people and creatures rendered vulnerable by the blizzard and lead us all to safety. ***Amen***. (*Anne Rowthorn*)[88]

PSALM 147:7–9, 16–18

Sing to our God with thanksgiving;
sing praise with the harp to our God—

who covers the heavens with clouds,
and provides rain for the earth,

who makes grass sprout on the mountains
and herbs for the service of the people

who gives food to the cattle,
and to the young ravens when they cry. . . .

God spreads snow like wool,
and scatters frost like ashes.

God hurls hail like pebbles—
who can stand before God's freezing winds?

Then God sends a word and melts them;
God lets the breeze blow and the waters run again.[89]

SCRIPTURE JOB 37:2–13

"Listen, listen to the thunder of his voice
    and the rumbling that comes from his mouth.
Under the whole heaven he lets it loose,
    and his lightning to the corners of the earth.
After it his voice roars;
    he thunders with his majestic voice,
    and he does not restrain the lightnings when his voice is heard.

God thunders wondrously with his voice;
he does great things that we cannot comprehend.
For to the snow he says, 'Fall on the earth';
and the shower of rain, his heavy shower of rain,
serves as a sign on everyone's hand,
so that all whom he has made may know it.
Then the animals go into their lairs
and remain in their dens.
From its chamber comes the whirlwind
and cold from the scattering winds.
By the breath of God ice is given,
and the broad waters are frozen fast.
He loads the thick cloud with moisture;
the clouds scatter his lightning.
They turn round and round by his guidance
to accomplish all that he commands them
on the face of the habitable world.
Whether for correction or for his land
or for love, he causes it to happen." (*NRSVue*)

LITANY ANNE ROWTHORN

As the driving snow gathers over the land and winter winds howl, we look to you for protection and we rest assured in the knowledge that all creation worships you, O holy Creator God of the universe:

Praise to you, Creator God.

O frozen earth and howling winds—

Praise to you, Creator God.

O swirling snow and brittle trees—

Praise to you, Creator God.

You sleet, hail, and driving rain—

Praise to you, Creator God.

You frost and cold and Arctic chill—

Praise to you, Creator God.

You stars and planets dancing across the winter sky—

Praise to you, Creator God.

O snow leopards and reindeer, you owls of the night—

Praise to you, Creator God.

You snakes in your pits, you bears slumbering in your dens—

Praise to you, Creator God.

You snowy hills and mountains, you frozen lakes and ponds—

Praise to you, Creator God.

You tides and waves crashing against the foamy shore—

Praise to you, Creator God.

All glory to you for covering the world in a blanket of deep peace.[90]

REFLECTION O. E. RØLVAAG

Per Hansa . . . had seen plenty of storms . . . , but nothing like this had ever before come within the range of their experience. Like lightning, a giant troll had risen up in the west, ripped open his great sack of woolly fleece, and emptied the whole contents of it above their heads.

A squall of snow so thick they could not see an arm's length ahead of them, a sucking noise, a few angry blasts, howling in fury, then dropping away to uncertain draughts of air that wandered idly here and there, swirling, . . . a sharp hissing sound mingled with growls like thunder—and then the blizzard broke in all its terror. . . .

The storm howled and whined, driving the snow before it like giant breakers. A grey-black spume enveloped them, a raging cloud. . . . Instinctively Per Hansa found himself peering through the murk. . . . God Almighty!

. . . His first impulse was to sink down where he stood, to snatch a moment's peace, to give in to the weariness that was overmastering him. But deep down within him a voice commanded him to keep on standing. . . . Per Hansa trembled so violently that he could hardly keep his feet. He saw [an] eye shining through the drifting snow that was the light from the small window in the log wall. He found his way around the house corner, came to a door, flung it open . . . and stumbled in. . . . [H]is face was crusted with snow and ice; his eyelashes were frozen together. . . . But he was conscious, with a deep sense of joy and relief that this was a safe place and that there were folk around him again.[91]

This reflection from the great American epic novel Giants in the Earth *describes the onset of a terrifying blizzard in the Dakota Territory when the main character was caught miles from home with his team of oxen. A Norwegian immigrant who worked as a farm hand in South Dakota in 1896, Rølvaag would have experienced Midwestern blizzards and he would have heard many accounts of the infamous 1888 School House Blizzard that came on so quickly it caught thousands unprepared and killed 235 people, mostly children, trying to return home from school.*

PRAYERS

Lord, in the midst of winter, when the days are cold and wind can pierce, remind us of the warmth of your love. In the midst of winter, when days are short, dawn comes late, and dusk arrives early, remind us that in the darkness your light still shines. In the midst of winter, when the flowers of spring still lie hidden in the earth, when leaves are off the trees, and the world can seem bleak, remind us that Easter is but a short time away. And when in our lives we feel as if we are experiencing a season of winter, reach out to us with the power of your resurrection so that we may feel the warmth of your love and see your light that alone can take away the darkness of our soul. ***Amen.*** *(Cal Wick)*[92]

May it be your will, O Lord our God and the God of our ancestors, that you lead us toward peace; guide our footsteps toward peace, and make us reach our desired destination for life, gladness, and peace. May you rescue us from the hand of every foe and ambush along the way. . . . May you send blessing on our handiwork, and grant us grace, kindness, and mercy in your eyes and in the eyes of all who see us. May you hear the sound of our humble request because you are God who hears our prayers. Blessed are you. ***Amen.*** *(Traditional Jewish prayer, author unknown)*[93]

9. Blizzard

HYMN SAMUEL LONGFELLOW

1. 'Tis winter now; the fallen snow
has left the heavens all coldly clear;
through leafless boughs the sharp winds blow,
and all the earth lies dead and drear.

2. And yet God's love is not withdrawn;
his life within the keen air breathes;
his beauty paints the crimson dawn,
and clothes each branch with glittering wreaths.

3. And though abroad the sharp winds blow,
and skies are chill, and frosts are keen,
home closer draws her circle now,
and warmer glows her light within.

4. O God, you give the winter's cold,
as well as summer's joyous rays,
you warmly in your love enfold,
and keep us through life's wintry days.[94]

Tune: ROCKINGHAM, 8.8.8.8

Following whatever roads the rainmakers mark out; may the ice blanket spread out, may the ice blanket cover the country. May the flesh of our Mother Earth crack open from the cold, that your thoughts may bend to this, that your words may be to this end.

For this with prayers I send you forth. *(Zuñi prayer, author unknown)*[95]

10. PETROLEUM PIPELINES

The 2.5 million miles of petroleum pipelines in the United States cross under thousands of rivers, lakes, and streams, including the Yellowstone River, which runs through iconic Yellowstone National Park. Two pipeline breaks have occurred in the Yellowstone River in recent years, and since 1986 pipeline accidents have killed five hundred people and injured four thousand.

Lord, sweeten the waters. Lord, sweeten the grass. Lord, sweeten and swell all the rivers. Lord, sweeten all animals. Lord, give us land. Lord, let the land be green. Lord, give us rains. Lord, give us fruitful lands. Lord, sweeten all rivers. ***Amen.*** *(Maasai prayer, author unknown)*[96]

PRAYERS

We give you thanks, most gracious God, for the beauty of earth and sky and sea; for the richness of mountains, plains, and rivers; for the songs of birds and the loveliness of flowers. We praise you for these good gifts, and we pray that we may safeguard them for posterity. Grant that we may continue to grow in our grateful enjoyment of your abundant creation, to the honor and glory of your name, now and forever. ***Amen.*** *(Episcopal Church)*[97]

Grandfather, Great Spirit, we thank you for this life. As you have taught us to honor our mother, the Earth, now help us show others how to respect your creation. Strengthen us as we stand up on your behalf to protest powerful interests in the fossil fuel industry. They are swaying government officials by their arguments as they plan to build pipelines across state and sacred tribal lands. Help us educate people about the catastrophic effects of an oil spill on rivers and the water supply for so many communities. Help us communicate well so that we can live in peace with all our brothers and sisters and all our relatives in the natural world. Protect us during our protests and protect our water and our sacred lands. ***Amen.*** *(Frederic and Mary Ann Brussat)*[98]

PSALM 136:1–9, 16–17, 21–22

O give thanks to the LORD, who is good,
for God's faithful love endures forever.

Give thanks to the God of gods,
for God's faithful love endures forever.

Give thanks to the Lord of lords,
for God's faithful love endures forever;

Who alone has wrought marvelous works,
for God's faithful love endures forever;

who in wisdom made the heavens,
for God's faithful love endures forever;

who spread the earth on the waters,
for God's faithful love endures forever.

It was the LORD who made the great lights,
for God's faithful love endures forever;

the sun to rule in the day,
for God's faithful love endures forever;

the moon and the stars in the night,
for God's faithful love endures forever. . . .

The LORD led the people through the desert,
for God's faithful love endures forever.

Kings in their greatness he struck down,
for God's faithful love endures forever. . . .

**The LORD gave their land as a heritage,
for God's faithful love endures forever,**

a heritage for Israel, God's servant,
for God's faithful love endures forever.[99]

SCRIPTURE EZEKIEL 47:7, 9–12

. . . I saw on the bank of the river a great many trees on one side and on the other. . . . "Wherever the river goes, every living creature that swarms will live, and there will be very many fish once these waters reach there. It will become fresh, and everything will live where the river goes. People will stand fishing beside the sea from En-gedi to En-eglaim; it will be a place for the spreading of nets; its fish will be of a great many kinds, like the fish of the Great Sea. But its swamps and marshes will not become fresh; they are to be left for salt. On the banks, on both sides of the river, there will grow all kinds of trees for food. Their leaves will not wither nor their fruit fail, but they will bear fresh fruit every month, because the water for them flows from the sanctuary. Their fruit will be for food and their leaves for healing." (*NRSVue*)

LITANY TWEEDY SOMBRERO NAVARRETE

We acknowledge that this land is the traditional territory of Indigenous Peoples. Their presence is imbued in the lands and waters surrounding us. May we nurture our relationship with our Indigenous neighbors, and our shared responsibilities for their homelands.

Thank you, Lord, for the people gathering around us now. Let us take this time to give thanks for these things of earth that give us the means of life.

Thank you for the natural world in which we find the means to be clothed and housed.

Thank you, Lord, for the ability to use these gifts of the natural world.

Help us to see our place among these gifts, not to squander them or think of them as means for selfish gain.

May we respect the life of all you have made.

May our spirit be strengthened by using only what we need and may we use our strength to help those who need us. Giver of life, in the midst of a plundered earth we groan with creation:

Have mercy on us.

Giver of life, in the midst of poisoned waters we groan with creation:

Have mercy on us.

Giver of life, in the midst of polluted air we groan with creation:

Have mercy on us.

Giver of life, in the midst of mountains of waste we groan with creation:

Have mercy on us.

Giver of life, we who are made in the image of God have gone astray. Attitudes of conquest and greed harm us all. Creation groans with us.

Have mercy on us.

Thank you, Lord, for all that you have given us. Thank you for the beauty of the universe that you created: the trees, the sky, the mountains, the rain and fresh water everywhere. All things hold beauty and all are related. You created the rhythm and pattern of the universe in a harmony of movement, sight, and sound. Help us to appreciate your creation and to live with our eyes, ears, and hearts open to your message.[100]

REFLECTION MARK TRAHANT

America has more than 2.5 million miles of oil and gas pipelines crossing the country in every direction. So plans to construct the 1,172-mile Dakota Access Pipeline from oil fields in North Dakota through South Dakota and Iowa to Patoka, Illinois, were supposed to be a nonevent. The regulatory process was largely conducted through state commissions and the US Army Corps of Engineers and was far less stringent than the successfully opposed Keystone XL pipeline. Just one more pipeline. . . .

The Standing Rock Sioux Tribe objected. The pipeline route threatens the tribe's drinking water and would disturb sacred and cultural sites, and so the tribal government has opposed the project since 2014. . . .

The Standing Rock Sioux Tribe clearly has the moral high ground. An earlier proposal for the pipeline to cross the Missouri River north of Bismarck, North Dakota, was scrapped because it threatened the capital's water supply. So the very decision to move the route south was to sacrifice Native communities. A decade ago, even a couple of years ago, that might have worked, but not in this era of social media. People of goodwill easily recognize this injustice. . . .

Once there was a case to be made for pipelines, but that moment was in our history and is now irrelevant.[101]

Mark Trahant, a member of the Shoshone-Bannock Tribe, is a journalism professor at the University of North Dakota. Led by members of the Standing Rock Tribe, a diverse group of thousands of tribal members and indigenous people from around the world—environmentalists, human rights advocates, and religious leaders—staged a series of prayerful protests to halt the construction of the Dakota Access Pipeline.

PRAYERS

We remember the dry land that rose from the waters in the beginning of creation, and the plants that emerged from the soil. We remember with delight the gardens and the fields of our childhood, the places where we played in the sand, when we felt close to the ground. Thank you, God, for the land, for water, for soils that sustain our life. We remember and confess we have not loved and respected the land of our garden planet. We are sorry. We have killed living soils with excessive use of chemicals. We have turned fertile fields into lifeless salt plains. We have polluted sacred waters. We have cleared rich lands of wild life. We have swallowed earth's resources in selfish cities. We are sorry! We are sorry! ***Amen.*** (*Season of Creation)*[102]

Eternal Spirit, Earth-maker, Pain-bearer, Life-giver, Source of all that is and that shall be, Father and Mother of us all, Loving God, in whom is heaven: The hallowing of your name echoes through the universe! The way of your justice be followed by the peoples of the world! Your heavenly will be done by all created beings! Your commonwealth of peace and freedom sustain our hope and come on earth. With the bread we need for today, feed us. In the hurts we absorb from one another, forgive us. In times of temptations and testing, strengthen us. From trials too great to endure, spare us. From the grip of all that is evil, free us. For you reign in the glory of the power that is love, now and forever. ***Amen.*** *(Jim Cotter)*[103]

HYMN SHIRLEY ERENA MURRAY

1. Touch the earth lightly,
use the earth gently,
nourish the life of the world in our care:
gift of great wonder,
ours to surrender,
trust for the children tomorrow will bear.

2. We who endanger,
who create hunger,
agents of death for all creatures that live,
we who still foster
clouds of disaster,
God of our planet, forestall and forgive!

3. Let there be greening,
birth from the burning,
water that blesses, and air that is sweet,
health in God's garden,
hope in God's children,
regeneration that peace will complete.

4. God of all living,
God of all loving,
God of the seedling, the snow, and the sun,
teach us, deflect us,
Christ, reconnect us,
using us gently and making us one.[104]

Tune: TENDERNESS, 5.5.10 D. Words © 1992 Hope Publishing

The world now is too dangerous and too beautiful for anything but love. May your eyes be so blessed you see God in everyone; your ears, so you hear the cry of the poor. May your hands be so blessed that everything you touch is a sacrament; your lips, so you speak nothing but the truth with love. May your feet be so blessed you run to those who need you. And may your heart be so opened, so set on fire, that your love changes everything. ***Amen.*** *(Brian Baker)*[105]

11. OCEAN OIL SPILLS

Covering two-thirds of earth's surface, oceans are where life on our planet first evolved. Oceans support a vast diversity of species, and they are essential in stabilizing the planet's climate. Even small changes in oceanic salinity and temperature can adversely affect weather patterns. Damage to the seas through off-shore drilling, oil spills, and dumping harms not only the seas and marine life, but the wellbeing of all earth.

So God created the great sea monsters and every living creature that moves, of every kind, with which the waters swarm and every winged bird of every kind. And God saw that it was good. *(Genesis 1:21 NRSVue)*

PRAYERS

God our Creator, as we reflect on the mysteries of the ocean depths, we celebrate the wondrous design of the seas that surround us. Help us to discern how we have polluted our oceans and to empathize with the groaning of creation beneath us. Teach us to sense the presence of God in the tides and currents of the surging seas. Teach us to care for the oceans and all our waterways. In the name of the Wisdom of God, the creative force that designs and governs all creation. ***Amen.*** *(Season of Creation)*[106]

We remember and confess that we have killed reefs, polluted seas, and turned surrounding oceans into domains to be conquered. We are sorry. We have polluted earth's waters with toxins, and killed millions of species in the ocean. We have turned our greed into global warming. We have helped cause arctic regions to melt. We have loved progress more than the planet. We are sorry. We are sorry. ***Amen.*** *(Season of Creation)*[107]

PSALM 104:1–3, 24–28

Bless the Lord, O my soul.
    O Lord my God, you are very great.

You are clothed with honor and majesty,
    wrapped in light as with a garment.

You stretch out the heavens like a tent;
    you set the beams of your chambers on the waters;

you make the clouds your chariot;
    you ride on the wings of the wind . . .

O Lord, how manifold are your works!
    In wisdom you have made them all;
    the earth is full of your creatures.

There is the sea, great and wide;
    creeping things innumerable are there,
    living things both small and great.

There go the ships,
    and Leviathan that you formed to sport in it.

These all look to you
    to give them their food in due season;

when you give to them, they gather it up;
    when you open your hand, they are filled with good things. (*NRSVue*)

SCRIPTURE JOB 38:4–11

"Where were you when I laid the foundation of the earth?
    Tell me, if you have understanding.
Who determined its measurements—surely you know!
    Or who stretched the line upon it?
On what were its bases sunk,
    or who laid its cornerstone

when the morning stars sang together
    and all the heavenly beings shouted for joy?

"Or who shut in the sea with doors
    when it burst out from the womb,
when I made the clouds its garment
    and thick darkness its swaddling band,
and prescribed bounds for it,
    and set bars and doors,
and said, 'Thus far shall you come and no farther,
    and here shall your proud waves be stopped'?" (*NRSVue*)

LITANY FREDERIC AND MARY ANN BRUSSAT

I am the ocean, mighty, wild, and free and I am being poisoned with oil. From a hole humans drilled into the earth's skin flows a stream I cannot stop, threatening all I shelter.

Breath to breath, body to body, we are One. So be it.

I am a worker injured in the oil spill and I worry about the safety of the oil industry. I want to know why the regulations and procedures that were supposed to protect us failed.

Breath to breath, body to body, we are One. So be it.

I am part of the crew cleaning up this mess. I am tired and frustrated that the leak is not stopped. I feel sick from the fumes of the oil and the chemicals used to disperse it.

Breath to breath, body to body, we are One. So be it.

I am a fisherman, a fisherwoman and I worry about my livelihood. Vast areas of the ocean are closed to fishing, and now oil is creeping into the estuaries and marshlands that serve as fish and shrimp nurseries.

Breath to breath, body to body, we are One. So be it.

I am a wildlife rescue person and I want to save the lives of as many innocent creatures as I can. I am heartbroken at what I am seeing in the oil-slick waters and hope the affected populations can recover.

Breath to breath, body to body, we are One. So be it.

I am a dolphin used to swimming freely around the ocean oil rigs, but now when I dive and surface I must go through layers of oil. My pod and I cannot get away from it.

Breath to breath, body to body, we are One. So be it.

I am a pelican, my habitat has been contaminated so that it is no longer safe for me to raise my family on it. My feathers are completely covered with oil, and I cannot clean them by myself.

Breath to breath, body to body, we are One. So be it.

I am a sea turtle and the sea I swim in and the beaches I frequent are saturated with oil. I wonder how my kind can survive this calamity.

Breath to breath, body to body, we are One. So be it.

I am a fish, a crab, a shrimp. My environment has turned into a toxic soup of oil and chemicals, and I am having trouble breathing in the waters I call home.

Breath to breath, body to body, we are One. So be it.

I am just a tiny organism in the deep sea plankton, an important part of the food chain for sea creatures. I am being smothered by oil sinking to the bottom of the ocean.

Breath to breath, body to body, we are One. So be it.

I am an inhabitant of the earth. I want things to change and change begins with me. This deep-sea oil spill is for me both a painful tragedy and a teachable moment.

Breath to breath, body to body, we are One. So be it.[108]

REFLECTION ANNE PLATT MCGINN

From the Greeks in the Mediterranean to the Chinese in the Yellow Sea, marine environments have provided the backbone for food security, commerce, trade, and transportation for centuries. Ancient civilizations sprang up on coasts of inland seas and oceans where fish were abundant. . . . Archaeological evidence from the western Pacific reveals that *Homo erectus* began building boats as far back as eight hundred thousand years ago, suggesting that people turned to the sea for food long before agricultural fields were plowed. . . .

Oceans are vital to both the chemical and biological balance of life. The same mechanism that created the present atmosphere—photosynthesis—continues today to feed the marine food chain. Phytoplankton—tiny microscopic plants—take carbon dioxide from the atmosphere and convert it to oxygen and simple sugars, a form of carbon that can be consumed by marine animals. . . .

In 1967, . . . the Liberian oil tanker Torrey Canyon ran aground off Britain's southwest coast dumping 120,000 tons of crude oil. The largest in a series of highly visible disasters brought the horror of marine pollution to headlines worldwide and helped spark international action. . . .

For generations, oceans have drawn people to their shores for a glimpse of the horizon, a sense of scale and awe at nature's might. Today, oceans offer a different kind of awe: a warning that our impacts on the earth are exceeding natural bounds and in danger of disrupting life. . . . How we choose to react will determine the future of the planet. . . . Oceans are not simply one more system under pressure—they are critical to our survival.[109]

Anne Platt McGinn writes about oceans. Her articles include "Safeguarding the Health of Oceans" and "Rocking the Boat: Conserving Fisheries and Protecting Jobs." Since the Torrey Canyon disaster, international organizations have mandated that petroleum tankers be constructed with double-hulls, and instituted tighter clean-up procedures. Nonetheless, oil tanker ships remain a problem, along with spills from off-shore drilling.

PRAYERS

God of oceans and estuaries and waterways everywhere: we pray for the cod and the tuna, for dolphins, great whales, stingrays, sharks, and all fish of the oceans—their only home. We pray for the pelicans, seagulls, cormorants, and sandpipers—our brother and sister birds now covered in oil. We pray for the sea turtles who migrate along the oil slick; for clams and mussels, starfish, snails, and sea urchins. We pray for all marine animals, for plankton, sea grasses, and seaweed—every marine animal and plant intimately connected in the web of life. If they loose their links with each other and with the water and their connection with us in the human community, we know we will ultimately destroy ourselves. We pray for our sister oceans and for the vibrant life contained therein and we pledge to work against all that would harm and destroy them. This we ask in of name of Jesus, who, with his disciples, fished the Sea of Galilee. ***Amen.*** *(Anne Rowthorn)*[110]

Swirling God, who at the dawn of creation swept over the face of the waters, hover over our oceans and all waterways with your blessed presence. May each droplet of mist and sea be clean and fresh for all life who come in contact with these holy streams. Bless each cell and molecule of life below the surface of the waters who trust in you and us to create a healthy world. Continually nudge us to nurture creation, joining together with humans all over this planet to covenant with one another and celebrate the gifts of water, air, fire, and land that you have given us. ***Amen.*** *(Michelle L. Torigian)*[111]

HYMN NORMAN HABEL

1. Watch once more the windswept storm clouds;
suddenly the sky has wings!
God has come among us,
giving hope to all dry things.
Sing a song of splashing waters,
pulsing through the veins of earth.

2. Taste the moisture of the morning,
smoother than the best red wine;
toast the lifeblood of the planet:
here's to God's wild wet design!
Sing a song of flowing waters,
pulsing through the veins of earth.

3. View anew the dark blue ocean,
whales cavorting, spraying foam;
God at play with deep sea monsters,
feeling very much at home.
Sing a song of laughing waters,
pulsing through the veins of earth.

4. Feel the breath of God move softly,
gentle mists that brush the skin;
earth is breathing God's own Spirit,

life renewed from deep within.
Sing a song of living waters,
pulsing through the veins of earth.[112]

Tune: LAUDA ANIMA, 87.87.87

May God who parted the waters so the Israelites could pass through in safety to dry land, keep us and all the sacred waters of earth and sea safe and clean, and may our hopes and prayers for our island home rise with the rhythm of the everlasting waves. *(Anne Rowthorn)*[113]

12. MELTDOWN

When the atom was split almost a century ago, a whole new energy source was uncovered, powerful beyond the range of human imagining. It both dazzles and frightens. It gave us Bikini Atoll, Hiroshima, Nagasaki, Chernobyl, and Fukushima. Used peacefully, nuclear energy is a major power source in the USA, France, China, and Russia. Can a new generation of nuclear power plants be made safer?

O God, great and wonderful, who has created the heavens, dwelling in their light and beauty and who has made the earth, revealing yourself on every flower that opens: let not our eyes be blind to you, neither let our hearts be dead, but teach us to praise you, even as the lark which offers her song at daybreak. (*St. Isidore of Seville*)[114]

PRAYERS

Loving God, come now and make us into a global neighborhood, looking out for each other through struggle and crisis and reaching out to strangers who become sisters and brothers. Shape us into a caring community, strengthening each other through every challenge and standing together until justice comes for all. ***Amen.*** (*Christian Aid, UK*)[115]

God of healing and mercy, we come before you with our hearts filled with grief as we see the devastation. We pray that your presence will be felt by those who are grieving, those who are injured, those who have lost their homes and livelihoods. We pray for wisdom and safety for those who are responding to people in need and the many challenges left in the wake of nuclear accidents. We pray for our church, that it may be a witness to your compassion and care for all who suffer. God, you are our refuge and strength, an ever-present help in times of trouble. For this we give you thanks and ask that you hear our prayers for all people in need (and particularly the people of ___________). ***Amen.*** (*Angelika Dawson*)[116]

PSALM 90:1–6, 13–17

Lord, you have been our dwelling place
in all generations.

Before the mountains were brought forth
or ever you had formed the earth and the world,
from everlasting to everlasting you are God.

You turn us back to dust
and say, "Turn back, you mortals."

For a thousand years in your sight
are like yesterday when it is past
or like a watch in the night.

You sweep them away; they are like a dream,
like grass that is renewed in the morning;

in the morning it flourishes and is renewed;
in the evening it fades and withers. . . .

Turn, O LORD! How long?
Have compassion on your servants!

Satisfy us in the morning with your steadfast love,
so that we may rejoice and be glad all our days.

Make us glad as many days as you have afflicted us
and as many years as we have seen evil.

Let your work be manifest to your servants,
and your glorious power to their children.

Let the favor of the Lord our God be upon us
and prosper for us the work of our hands—
O prosper the work of our hands! (*NRSVue*)

SCRIPTURE 2 CORINTHIANS 4:8–18

We are afflicted in every way but not crushed, perplexed but not driven to despair, persecuted but not forsaken, struck down but not destroyed, always carrying around in the body the death of Jesus, so that the life of Jesus may also be made visible in our bodies. For we who are living are always being handed over to death for Jesus's sake, so that the life of Jesus may also be made visible in our mortal flesh. So death is at work in us but life in you.

But just as we have the same spirit of faith that is in accordance with scripture—"I believed, and so I spoke"—we also believe, and therefore we also speak, because we know that the one who raised Jesus will also raise us with Jesus and will present us with you in his presence. Indeed, everything is for your sake, so that grace, as when it has extended to more and more people, may increase thanksgiving, to the glory of God.

So we do not lose heart. Even though our outer nature is wasting away, our inner nature is being renewed day by day. For our slight, momentary affliction is producing for us for an eternal weight of glory beyond all measure, because we look not at what can be seen but at what cannot be seen, for what can be seen is temporary, but what cannot be seen is eternal. (*NRSVue*)

LITANY DIANA MACALINTAL

Lord, at times such as this, when we realize that the ground beneath our feet is not as solid as we had imagined,

we plead for your mercy.

As the things we have built crumble about us, we know too well how small we truly are on this ever-changing, ever-moving, fragile planet we call home. Yet you have promised never to forget us.

Do not forget us now.

Today, so many people are afraid. They hear the cries of the injured amid the rubble. They roam the streets in shock at what they see. And they fill the dusty air with wails of grief and the names of missing dead.

Comfort them, Lord, in this disaster.

Be their rock when the nuclear plant melts down, and shelter them under your wings when homes and businesses no longer exist.

Shelter them under your wings.

Embrace in your arms those who died so suddenly this day. Console the hearts of those who mourn, and ease the pain of bodies on the brink of death.

Embrace them, Lord.

Pierce, too, our hearts with compassion for we know the living fear of radiation sickness that is bound to follow this tragedy,

and we pray unceasingly for those without hope.

And once the nuclear dust has settled, the images of destruction have stopped filling the news, let us not forget that we are all your children and they are our brothers and sisters.

We are all the work of your hands.

For though the mountains leave their place and the hills be tossed to the ground and the soil forever poisoned, your love shall never leave us, and your promise of peace will never be shaken.

Our help is in the name of the Lord, who made heaven and earth. Blessed be the name of the Lord, now and forever.[117]

REFLECTION SUBRATA GHOSHROY

We arrived at Namie, our destination, and as close as we could get to the actual plant itself. . . . Namie had a population of twenty-one thousand before it was evacuated. About fourteen thousand were relocated within Fukushima prefecture and six thousand outside. Two hundred people were known to have perished [here] in the tsunami. Baba Isao [Assemblyman for the town] . . . said that some people wanted to return, but he had advised them against it. . . . The government was making Namie's clean-up a priority, undertaking infrastructure improvement and house-to-house decontamination. The town was considering a proposal that would allow people to return . . . but Isao was doubtful.

In addition to the presence of radiation, there was another reason not to return: There were no longer any jobs in these communities, where the nuclear power plant was the *raison d'être* for the town. In fact, before the accident, in a bid to boost the economy, the town had been negotiating with the Tohoku Electric Power Company to set up another nuclear plant in Namie.

We found a perfect ghost town where life ceased to exist, as if a light switch had been turned off. Abandoned homes were now inhabited by cats. In the downtown area there were closed stores, including a barbershop and a bakery. All looked as if the employees were on a break. There were tens of bikes left at the train station; a few buses were parked in their designated spots as if waiting for commuters to disembark from a train.

We drove through more silent streets before arriving at an elementary school, which had been in the tsunami's path. The school building was destroyed, but the children miraculously survived by running to a hill nearby. Inside the building, there were children's lockers with small boxes for crayons. A memorial *stupa*—a mound-like, Buddhist shrine—stood on the roadside, with flowers and candles.

From the elementary school, we could just barely see what appeared to be the top of the turbine buildings of the Fukushima Daiichi plant. Red and white construction cranes hovered over them. Namie escaped more damage thanks to the prevailing winds, which dispersed much of the fallout toward the ocean. And what if that second nuclear plant had already been up and running when disaster struck? Ironically, Namie had been lucky. Things could have been much worse.[118]

The Fukushima Daiichi nuclear accident occurred when waves from the tsunami overwhelmed and disabled emergency generators. Beautiful historic fishing villages and nearby farming communities were destroyed. One hundred thousand people were evacuated and between one thousand and one thousand six hundred people perished from radiation sickness. Five years after the accident, a small group from the Japan Scientists Association received permission for a guided tour of the area surrounding the Fukushima Daiichi plant. Subrata Ghoshroy, who shares this reflection, is a professor at Tokyo Institute of Technology and was a member of the group.

PRAYERS

We repent that our lives have caused catastrophic problems for the environment and have threatened the survival of all humankind by indiscreet use of nuclear energy. We repent that we have turned blind eyes and stopped our ears to the dangers of nuclear power generation despite the warning from Fukushima. We pray that we can turn from the road of nuclear power generation, which can be disastrous. We pray that a world of peace may be realized and the dignity of life protected as we convert nuclear energy into renewable natural energy. We pray that the world's Christians may abandon the catastrophe of nuclear weapons and power plants and instead walk together toward the path of peace for all. ***Amen.*** (*Pastors in Busan, South Korea)*[119]

O gracious God who knows all our needs and who cares for us daily with such great love, be with all who are affected by this tragedy, all who are in great need of your presence right now. May you light surround us (them); may your love be our (their) support, and may your life flow through us (them). We dedicate the actions, prayers and duties of this day for our (their) special needs at this time. ***Amen.*** *(Edward Hays)*[120]

HYMN JOACHIM NEANDER

1. All my hope on God is founded;
he doth still my trust renew.
Me through change and chance he guideth,
only good and only true.
God unknown,
he alone
calls my heart to be his own.

2. Human pride and earthly glory,
sword and crown betray his trust;
what with care and toil he buildeth,
tower and temple, fall to dust.
But God's power,
hour by hour,
is my temple and my tower.

3 God's great goodness aye endureth,
deep his wisdom, passing thought:
splendor, light, and life attend him,
beauty springeth out of naught.
Evermore
from his store
new-born worlds rise and adore.

4. Daily doth th' Almighty giver
bounteous gifts on us bestow;
his desire our soul delighteth,
pleasure leads us where we go.
Love doth stand
at his hand;
joy doth wait on his command.

5. Still from earth to God eternal
sacrifice of praise be done,
high above all praises praising
for the gift of Christ his Son.
Christ doth call
one and all:
ye who follow shall not fall.[121]

Tune: MICHAEL, 87.87.337

May God look upon us with kindness, and give us peace. May the God of all consolation bless us in every way and grant us peace all the days of our lives. ***Amen***. *(Author unknown)*[122]

13. PANDEMIC

A pandemic strips off society's veneer, revealing both its cracks and strengths. It makes everyday heroes of those who keep the food supply running, supermarket shelves stocked, and the sick lovingly cared for. We respond with great gratitude.

"Come to me, all you who are weary and are carrying heavy burdens, and I will give you rest. Take my yoke upon you, and learn from me, for I am gentle and humble in heart, and you will find rest for your souls. For my yoke is easy, and my burden is light." *(Matthew 11:28–30 NRSVue)*

PRAYERS

Our spirits hunger for your love, for your joy and peace. May this time of prayer fill us with your presence and let us feel the touch of your hand upon our hearts. How we long for the depths of your love, to know your quiet constancy, the feast of your friendship that feeds us without end. Our souls long for you, you who elude all names we give you. Your essence pulses within every atom yet extends beyond the far frontiers of space: awaken us to your presence now, this moment, in our hearts. ***Amen.*** *(Edward Hays)*[123]

Loving God, divine source of health, wholeness, and compassion: behold your fearful people all over the world. Let your ear be attentive to our cries as we pray for all who are affected by the virus: for all healthcare-givers, for hospital and nursing home staff who have close contact with patients, and for the patients themselves. We pray for long-distance truck drivers who keep the food supply running; for all who handle money—bankers, supermarket and village market and convenience store cashiers; for all who pump gas; for restaurant workers, especially those who have lost their jobs; for daycare center staff who cuddle and comfort children and for all children; for teachers and professors, coaches and cafeteria workers at schools and universities across the world, and for students at home struggling to learn remotely; for the vulnerable, migrants, and the isolated elderly who have no protectors; for all who have died in the pandemic and are now free from pain and suffering. May the God of hope carry them all the way home, and comfort their families and friends. We pray out of the depths to you, O God of hope and expectation. ***Amen***. (*Anne and Jeffery Rowthorn)*[124]

PSALM 91:1–7, 9–16

You who . . . abide in the shadow of the Almighty,
will say to the LORD, "My refuge and my fortress;
 my God, in whom I trust."

For he will deliver you from the snare of the hunter
 and from the deadly pestilence;

he will cover you with his pinions,
 and under his wings you will find refuge;
 his faithfulness is a shield and defense.

You will not fear the terror of the night
 or the arrow that flies by day
or the pestilence that stalks in darkness
 or the destruction that wastes at noonday.

A thousand may fall at your side,
 ten thousand at your right hand,
 but it will not come near you. . . .

Because you have made the LORD your refuge,
 the Most High your dwelling place,
no evil shall befall you,
 no scourge come near your tent.

For he will command his angels concerning you
 to guard you in all your ways.

On their hands they will bear you up,
so that you will not dash your foot against a stone.

You will tread on the lion and the adder;
the young lion and the serpent you will trample under foot.

Those who love me, I will deliver;
I will protect those who know my name.

When they call to me, I will answer them;
I will be with them in trouble;
I will rescue them and honor them.

With long life I will satisfy them
and show them my salvation. (*NRSVue*)

SCRIPTURE REVELATION 21:1–6, 7B

Then I saw new heavens and a new earth. The former heavens and the former earth had passed away, and the sea existed no longer. I also saw a new Jerusalem, the holy city coming down out of heaven from God, beautiful as a bride and groom on their wedding day. And I heard a loud voice calling from the throne, "Look! God's tabernacle is among humankind! God will live with them; they will be God's people, and God will be fully present among them. The Most High will wipe away every tear from their eyes. And death, mourning, crying, and pain will be no more, for the old order has fallen." The One who sat upon the throne said, "Look! I am making everything new!" and added, "Write this, for what I am saying is trustworthy and true." And the One continued, "It is finished. I am the Alpha and the Omega, the Beginning and the End. To those who are thirsty I will give drink freely from the spring of the water of life. . . . I will be their God and they will be my daughters and sons."[125]

LITANY ANNE AND JEFFERY ROWTHORN

Creator God of the universe, God of a thousand names and faces; in your mercy we implore you to hear the cries of the broken-hearted and the crushed in Spirit. As we struggle to understand, you teach us that for everything there is a season, and a time for everything under heaven:

a time to break down, a time to weep, a time to die, a time to keep silence, and always, a time to love. During this sad season of the pandemic, we pray to you, confident that you will hear us in our distress . . .

For all who are sick at home, in hospitals, field hospitals, nursing homes, and waiting for treatment in emergency rooms. God is near to the broken-hearted—

and saves the crushed in Spirit.

For all who are dying in hospitals alone, denied visits from family members. God is near to the broken-hearted—

and saves the crushed in Spirit.

For those who have died, now free from every trace of illness; may they be held in the embrace of God who wipes away every pain and sorrow and leads the departed all the way home. God is near to the broken-hearted—

and saves the crushed in Spirit.

For the husbands, wives, and partners who are deprived of one final visit, one final look and feel, one final embrace, one final opportunity to say one last time, "I love you." God is near to the broken-hearted—

and saves the crushed in Spirit.

For the children of the dying, robbed of the opportunity to say, "Thank you, Mom." "Thank you, Dad." "You will be forever in our hearts." God is near to the broken-hearted—

and saves the crushed in Spirit.

For all who grieve their departed loved ones, especially those separated by distance. God is near to the broken-hearted—

and saves the crushed in Spirit.

For family members who suffer due to their inability to plan funerals and bury their dead, God is near to the broken-hearted—

and saves the crushed in Spirit.

13. Pandemic

Holy God of the universe: we cry out to you for help, and we pray that you will rescue us from all our troubles and bring about an end to this pandemic. Be with us as we long for a time of healing, a time to build up, a time to laugh, a time to dance, a time to embrace, and a time for peace. We pray out of the depths of our hearts to you, God of the broken-hearted and the crushed in Spirit, God of hope, whom we call Jesus, Allah, YHWH, Divine Mystery, Wakan Tanka, Great Spirit.[126]

REFLECTION ANNE ROWTHORN

We came to the Collegeville Institute in January to write hymns and articles, prayers and litanies, to give and attend seminars, and to read and worship. We have done some of that, but not nearly enough. Our lives—along with those of everyone else—have been completely overtaken by the collective trauma we are living through. I suppose we've learned something and as the days and weeks and months unfold, more may become clear.

I think we're appreciating each other more—friends, colleagues, family. Perhaps we are kinder, more loving and more deeply appreciative of each other. I think I am beginning to understand more fully how profoundly we are all connected with each other and the earth and all its systems. For me, I have felt the grounding, the beauty, and the security of the natural world more than ever. The geese and ducks, squirrels and rabbits don't know that the human world is suffering. The plants and grass and trees are screaming with fresh vibrancy. They weren't told we are in the midst of a plague.

In the distance Interstate 94 roars, cutting through the monastery lands. It is full of tractor trailers, serving as another reminder of the many ways we are connected and of the everyday heroes that keep daily life going.

This is Memorial Day, the day we honor the sacrifices of all people who have died in all our wars. They are mothers and fathers, aunts and uncles, and grandparents and brothers and sisters and cousins who once walked this earth loving and being loved, and finally paying the ultimate price. What haunts me is that there are also almost 100,000 people who have perished due to COVID-19. I would like to see a national day of mourning for them. I would like us to hold in our hearts all their family members, friends, and colleagues, who mourn their loss, and all their caregivers who were with them to the end.

Yes, today is beautiful. As Thoreau reminds us, "It's not what we look at that matters. It's what we see." The music of earth with its intricate web of relationships and connections is still beautiful and wonder-filled.[127]

During the first season of COVID, Anne and Jeffery Rowthorn, the compilers of this collection, kept a daily journal while they were residential scholars at the Collegeville Institute at St. John's Abbey and University in Collegeville, Minnesota.

PRAYERS

Brothers and sisters, we gather here in the protective shelter of God's healing love. This is a time to voice both memories and questions with one another and with God. We are free to grieve, to be angry or sad, and to know that God cares. We gather here as God's people, conscious of others who have died and of the frailty of our own existence on earth. We come to comfort and to support one another in our loss. We gather to hear God's word of hope that can diminish our despair and move us to offer God our praise. We gather to commend to God with thanksgiving all whom we grieve today as we celebrate the good news of Christ's resurrection. For whether we live or whether we die, we belong to God. ***Amen.*** (*Patty Jenkins*)[128]

Sacred Spirit, you are revealed to us in the sights, sounds, and smells of the creation which surrounds us and gives us life. Our life, all life, depends upon you. Help us now, in this time of grief, to rely upon you anew. Bless us with the comfort of your presence as we give thanks for the lives of all who have died and as we express sorrow at their death. Let the warmth of your love enfold us and give us peace. ***Amen***. (*Robyn Brown-Hewitt*)[129]

HYMN HENRY FRANCIS LYTE

1. Abide with me: fast falls the eventide;
the darkness deepens; Lord, with me abide.
When other helpers fail and comforts flee,
Help of the helpless, O abide with me.

2. Swift to its close ebbs out life's little day;
earth's joys grow dim, its glories pass away.

Change and decay in all around I see.
O thou who changest not, abide with me.

3. I need thy presence every passing hour.
What but thy grace can foil the tempter's power?
Who like thyself my guide and strength can be?
Through cloud and sunshine, O abide with me.

4. I fear no foe with thee at hand to bless,
ills have no weight, and tears no bitterness.
Where is death's sting? Where, grave, thy victory?
I triumph still, if thou abide with me.

5. Hold thou thy cross before my closing eyes.
Shine through the gloom and point me to the skies.
Heaven's morning breaks and earth's vain shadows flee;
in life, in death, O Lord, abide with me.[130]

Tune: EVENTIDE, 10.10.10.10

May the Christ who walks on wounded feet
walk with you on the road.
May the Christ who serves with wounded hands
stretch out your hands to serve.
May the Christ who loves with a wounded heart
open your hearts to love.
May you see the face of Christ in everyone you meet,
and may everyone you meet see the face of Christ in you. ***Amen.*** *(Celtic blessing)*[131]

14. DIVIDED NATION

The United States has always been a nation divided: divided over the Civil War, women's suffrage, whether or not to enter World Wars I and II, Vietnam, gay and women's rights, civil rights, rights to abortion, Second Amendment and gun rights, immigration, prayer in public schools, the place of religion in society, and the meaning of the common good. The challenge is that our nation not be overwhelmed by its divisions and that we seek a deeper unity in spite of everything. Our Pledge of Allegiance remains an ideal and a goal we are striving to achieve: that we will be "one nation under God, indivisible, with liberty, and justice for all."

"Every kingdom divided against itself is laid waste, and no city or house divided against itself will stand." *(Matthew 12:25 NRSVue)*

PRAYERS

Creator God of the universe, God of a thousand names and faces, God whose love knows no bounds: break down every barrier that divides the human family; take away every fear; crush all prejudice and suspicion of neighbor. Open wide the portals of hearts and minds and create in us a new spirit of openness and a new vision of the beloved community. Awaken in us the will to bring about a just society. This we ask in the name of God, the great reconciler. ***Amen.*** *(Anne and Jeffery Rowthorn)*[132]

Deepen and purify within us, O God, true and enlightened love for our country: a love that rejoices in beauty and ever seeks to preserve it; a love that could fill our land with happy homes; a love that will not rest until it has removed the stain of hopelessness and poverty and cured the blindness which passes it by. In the name of God who wept over his beloved Jerusalem, may we strive to make our country more worthy of God's love so that all people may live in peace and harmony. ***Amen.*** *(C. H. S. Matthews)*[133]

Creator who orders the universe, spark in us your fire for restorative justice in this broken world. Savior who embraces humanity, teach us to find you in each neighbor's face. Spirit who flows through all, let your peace like a powerful river burst forth from our hearts and actions. Trinity who dances in joyful communion, guide us together in your steps. ***Amen.*** *(Marie Hause)*[134]

PSALM 80:1–3, 8–15, 19

Give ear, O Shepherd of Israel,
you who lead Joseph like a flock!

You who are enthroned upon the cherubim, shine forth
before Ephraim and Benjamin and Manasseh.

Stir up your might,
and come to save us!

Restore us, O God;
let your face shine, that we may be saved. . . .

You brought a vine out of Egypt;
you drove out the nations and planted it.

You cleared the ground for it;
it took deep root and filled the land.

The mountains were covered with its shade,
the mighty cedars with its branches;

it sent out its branches to the sea,
and its shoots to the River.

Why then have you broken down its walls,
so that all who pass along the way pluck its fruit?

The boar from the forest ravages it,
and all that move in the field feed on it.

Turn again, O God of hosts;
look down from heaven and see;
have regard for this vine,

the stock that your right hand planted . . . .

Restore us, O LORD God of hosts;

let your face shine, that we may be saved. (*NRSVue*)

SCRIPTURE 2 CORINTHIANS 13:5–8, 11B–12

Examine yourselves to see whether you are living in the faith. Test yourselves. Do you not realize that Jesus Christ is in you?—unless, indeed, you fail to meet the test! I hope you will find out that we have not failed. But we pray to God that you may not do anything wrong—not that we may appear to have met the test but that you may do what is right, though we may seem to have failed. For we cannot do anything against the truth, but only for the truth. . . .

Be restored; listen to my appeal; agree with one another; live in peace; and the God of love and peace will be with you. Greet one another with a holy kiss. All the saints greet you. (*NRSVue*)

LITANY ALLA RENÉE BOZARTH

God of justice and hope, protect us from sinking into despair when our efforts to create justice come under attack.

Give us strength to raise our voices to speak for what is good and necessary.

Bless those who care for the poor, who share food with the hungry, who provide shelter for those needing refuge.

Renew our faith in the changing cycles of life so that we remember that bad times will give way to better times, and help us to do what we can to foster the good.

When human beings undermine peace by making lethal weapons available to violent people for the expression of resentment and rage,

inspire us with ways to help protect society, and especially children everywhere.

When the private lives of women and girls are put at risk by court declarations,

inspire us with ways to protect them and to restore the freedoms they have lost.

Help us to appreciate and respect those who hold differing convictions about when human life begins and how to protect it.

Human life is precious!

Help those whose task is to protect us from corrupt leaders by exposing their harmful intentions, and removing them from positions where they can do harm.

Help us to assign leadership to those who are worthy of it and who are intelligent, wise, and capable of leading the people in life-giving ways.

Holy One, teach us to balance patience with holy impatience for the restoration of justice,

so we can once again draw nearer to your dream and ours, for peace on earth and good will toward all.

You who are Spirit, Mother, Father, and Friend, be with us in ways that we can recognize, and when we cannot recognize your presence because of our distress, calm us and bring us back to our best selves, and into renewed and deeper awareness of you. ***Amen.***[135]

REFLECTION LAWRENCE FERLINGHETTI

Pity the nation whose people are sheep
and whose shepherds mislead them.
Pity the nation whose leaders are liars
whose sages are silenced
and whose bigots haunt the airwaves.

Pity the nation that raises not its voice
except to praise conquerors
and acclaim the bully as hero,
aiming to rule the world
by force and by torture.
Pity the nation that knows
no other language but its own
and no other culture but its own.
Pity the nation whose breath is money
and who sleeps the sleep of the too well fed.
Pity the nation, oh pity the people
who allow their rights to erode
and their freedoms to be washed away.
My country, tears of thee
Sweet land of liberty![136]

The poet and social activist Lawrence Ferlinghetti, who co-founded the celebrated City Lights Bookstore in San Francisco, was one of the Beat Generation activists which included Jack Kerouac, Allen Ginsberg, and Gary Snyder. In 2007 he rewrote a passage with the same title, "Pity the Nation," taken from the book, The Garden of the Prophet, *written in 1933 by philosopher of religion Kahlil Gibran.*

PRAYERS

May it come soon—to the hungry, to the weeping, to those who thirst for your justice, to those who have waited centuries for a truly human life. Grant us the patience to smooth the way on which your kingdom comes to us. Grant us hope that we may not be weary in proclaiming and working for it despite so many conflicts, threats, and shortcomings. Grant us a clear vision that in this hour of our history we may see the horizon and know the way by which your kingdom comes to us. ***Amen.*** *(Prayer from Nicaragua, author unknown)*[137]

Dear God, help us to rebuild this nation by seeking out your image in the face of others, finding the best in us to serve those who are the least, the lost, and the lonely. Help us to remember the words of one of your servants of old who reminded us that "perfect love casts out fear." Help us perfect our love. We are your people. You know us by many names. You are our God. We know you by many names. May we find strength in our diversity and seek the courage to live into what is written on every piece of currency in this nation: In God We Trust. In God. We Trust. For only in you can we live in safety. Only in you will we find justice. Only in you will we know the peace that passes all human understanding. ***Amen.*** *(Elizabeth Kaeton)*[138]

HYMN G. K. CHESTERTON

1. O God of earth and altar,
bow down and hear our cry,
our earthly rulers falter,
our people drift and die;
the walls of gold entomb us,
the swords of scorn divide,
take not thy thunder from us,
but take away our pride.

2. From all that terror teaches,
from lies of tongue and pen,
from all the easy speeches
that comfort cruel men,
from sale and profanation
of honor and the sword,
from sleep and from damnation,
deliver us, good Lord!

3. Tie in a living tether
the prince and priest and thrall,
bind all our lives together,
smite us and save us all;
in ire and exultation
aflame with faith, and free,
lift up a living nation,
a single sword to thee.[139]

Tune: KING'S LYNN, 7.6.7.6 D

Only humility will lead us to unity, and unity will lead us to peace. *(Mother Teresa)*[140]

15. GUN VIOLENCE

When twenty-eight children and educators were shot and killed at the Sandy Hook Elementary School in Newtown, Connecticut, on a pre-Christmas rampage in 2012, one might have thought the horror of six- and seven-year-olds brutally massacred would send shock waves throughout the country. Instead, there was a surge in gun sales, and gun violence continues to claim innocent victims in schools and movie theaters, clubs, offices, bars, and on city streets. Every day, 106 people in the USA are shot and killed.

Wherever justice is triumphing over the instincts of domination, wherever grace is winning out over the power of sin, . . . wherever love is getting the better of selfish interests, and whenever hope is resisting the lure of cynicism or despair, there the process of resurrection is being turned into reality. *(Leonardo Boff)*[141]

PRAYERS

Today we stand together to express our unity and our commitment. We stand as one people against the violence that has touched every corner of our country. And we commit ourselves to journey on the path toward a more perfect peace—peace in our hearts, in all of our homes, our towns and our cities—to a place where the sound of gunfire is stilled and the laughter of children fills the air. ***Amen.*** *(Jean Markey-Duncan)*[142]

O God who remembers, we hold before you all who have died from the plague of gun violence in our land. We remember those who have taken their lives with a gun, those who have died in school shootings and mass shootings, those who have died by a gun in the course of an argument or from abuse or by accident or during the commission of a crime. We lift our voices in sorrow and frustration, knowing that every life is infinitely valuable to you. Receive all who have died into the arms of your mercy, bless those who mourn with the hope of eternal life, and strengthen our hearts and our arms to bring an end to this scourge. This we pray in the name of the one who overcame the power of death, your Son, Jesus Christ. ***Amen.*** *(Bishops United Against Gun Violence)*[143]

PSALM 34:1, 4–5, 8, 18–19

I will bless the LORD at all times;
    his praise shall continually be in my mouth. . . .

I sought the LORD, and he answered me
    and delivered me from all my fears.

Look to him, and be radiant,
    so your faces shall never be ashamed. . . .

O taste and see that the LORD is good;
    happy are those who take refuge in him. . . .

The LORD is near to the brokenhearted,
    and saves the crushed in spirit.

Many are the afflictions of the righteous,
    but the LORD rescues us from them all. (*NRSVue*)

SCRIPTURE ISAIAH 2:2–4

In days to come
    the mountain of the LORD's house
shall be established as the highest of the mountains,
    and shall be raised above the hills;
all the nations shall stream to it.
    Many peoples shall come and say,
"Come, let us go up to the mountain of the LORD,
    to the house of the God of Jacob;

that he may teach us his ways
    and that we may walk in his paths."
For out of Zion shall go forth instruction,
    and the word of the LORD from Jerusalem.
He shall judge between the nations
    and shall arbitrate for many peoples;
they shall beat their swords into plowshares
    and their spears into pruning hooks;
nation shall not lift up sword against nation;
    neither shall they learn war any more. (*NRSVue*)

LITANY STEPHEN T. LANE

Giver of life and love, you created all people as one family and called us to live together in peace. Surround us with your love as we face again the tragedy of gun violence.

For the children and adults who were killed (___________), the brave ones who died protecting others, the many who were wounded and hospitalized, the traumatized, grieving survivors, and those known to you alone, Loving God,

Make us instruments of your peace.

God of righteousness, you have granted our leaders, especially our president, and our governors, the members of Congress and of our courts and legislatures, power and responsibility to protect us, and to uphold our right to life, liberty, and the pursuit of happiness. Strengthen their devotion to our common life and give them clarity of purpose.

For all who bear such responsibility, for all who struggle to discern what is right in the face of powerful political forces, Loving God,

Make us instruments of your peace.

God of compassion, we give you thanks for first responders: police officers, firefighters, EMTs, and all those whose duties bring them to the streets, the schools, the malls, and the homes where the carnage of gun violence takes place every day. Give them courage and sound judgment in the heat of the moment and grant them compassion for the victims.

For our brothers and sisters who risk their lives and serenity as they rush to our aid, Loving God,

Make us instruments of your peace.

Merciful God, bind up the wounds of all who suffer from gun violence, those maimed and disfigured, those left alone and grieving, and those who struggle to get through one more day. Bless them with your presence and help them find hope.

For all whose lives are forever changed and broken by the scourge of gun violence, Loving God,

Make us instruments of your peace.

God who remembers, may we not forget all those who have died in the past year in the gun violence that we have allowed to become routine. Receive them into your heart and comfort us with your promise of eternal love and care.

For all who have died, those who die today, and those who will die tomorrow, Loving God,

Make us instruments of your peace.

God of tender mercy, be with those who are overwhelmed, enraged, frustrated, and demoralized by the plague of gun violence. Give them a sense of your presence and plant in them the seed of hope.

For those whose hope for life in this world is shattered and broken, Loving God,

Make us instruments of your peace.

God of justice, give us courage to confront our false gods and to protest the needless deaths caused by gun violence. Help us rise above our dread that nothing can be done and grant us the conviction to advocate for change.

For your dream of a world where children are safe and all of us live together without fear, Loving God,

Make us instruments of your peace.

All this we pray in the name of the one who offered his life so that we might live, Jesus the Christ. ***Amen.***[144]

REFLECTION SARI KAUFMAN

February 14, it was Valentine's Day, and just like any other day, my mom dropped me off before school and I said, "Pick me up at this time," not thinking anything would happen. Go to school. I have a Spanish test that day. . . . Then I go to fourth period and I'm in my debate class. . . . The fire alarm goes off, and we are now a little uneasy just because why would we have two fire drills in a row? . . . And then, all of a sudden, we hear noises and we think it's gunshots, but it's Parkland and we always joke that nothing happens in Parkland because it's a quiet, safe town. . . . And then all of a sudden we see a police car driving on our baseball field going extremely fast and with their sirens on and it seems like all at the same moment we get text messages from our friends who are in the building where the shooting was occurring and saying, "My friend just got shot," and seeing videos. It was very surreal, but that's when we realized we're in a shooting and I just went into survival mode.

We just have to get out of the area and run as fast as we can. Administrators started running towards us, and police in SWAT gear starting to run towards us, and they just kept screaming, "Run, run, run." The police say, "We don't know where the shooter is, keep running."

So we keep running and we go to a local store, local restaurant, and we turn on the TV and it all still felt like I was in a dream. But once I looked at the TV . . . all of the major news outlets were saying first it was five dead at Marjory Stoneman Douglas High School and then ten dead. And it was obviously heartbreaking. And then when it's seventeen dead, it's just, it's un-comprehendible. And I was continuing to get texts from my family and friends, even numbers I didn't even know saying, "Are you okay?"

And I saw the community come together that day, just strangers helping strangers. . . .

After the shooting, it was, "Okay, this happened. What can we do? This is what we can do." So we went to Tallahassee; we lobbied legislators about gun violence prevention and what they can do to help us. And then after that it kind of transformed into, "Okay, we can have an event where we bring the whole entire country together." . . . It just pushes you and you come home to, "Okay, what can we do?"

A lot of times I think a lot of leaders kind of close out and only think what they can do, but I've learned, especially in our democracy, that it's about what the people can do.[145]

Eight months after the horrific Valentine's Day shooting at Marjorie Stoneman Douglas High School in Parkland, Florida, Sari Kaufman, a student, reflected on the rampage that left seventeen students and staff dead. The killer was a former student, a collector of knives and guns, who had legally purchased his semiautomatic rifle with multiple magazines.

PRAYERS

O God of mercy and grace, you bring hope in the midst of senseless tragedy and light in the midst of deepest darkness: we confess our need for the Risen Christ as we face into the realities of gun violence in the United States. We are mindful especially of the deaths in __________. So many children and adults have become fatal victims of people with access to powerful weapons.

We grieve with those loved ones who lost their lives in these shootings, and for so many in other shootings across this nation. We lift to your compassion, the injured, and pray for your healing grace. We beseech your presence to be with so many schoolchildren and area residents whose souls are scarred forever by these crimes. May you walk with them, dear Lord, in the valley of the shadow of death.

Deliver this nation, almighty God, from profound anxiety and anger. Help all of us to see your hand at work in the world about us. Release your Holy Spirit, O God, to put our full faith and trust in you. Let your peace which passes all understanding direct us to be peacemakers in time of anguish and sorrow. Bless us and sustain us now, and in every time of challenge, through Jesus Christ, the King of Peace. ***Amen.*** *(Anglican Fellowship of Prayer)*[146]

Loving God, when our world is engaged in darkness, we ask that you let us see your face shining in beauty in the lives of the good people around us. May you show us your face when we suffer; may you hide us in the cleft of a rock when storms are engulfing us so that we never lose touch with hope in you and in the beauty of the world and the people around us. We ask this through Christ our Lord. ***Amen.*** *(René McGraw)*[147]

HYMN CAROLYN WINFREY GILLETTE

1. God, we have heard it, sounding in the silence:
News of the children lost to this world's violence.
Children of promise! Then without a warning,
Loved ones are mourning.

2. Jesus, you came to bear our human sorrow;
You came to give us hope for each tomorrow.
You are our life, Lord God's own love revealing.
We need your healing!

3. Heal us from giving weapons any glory;
Help us, O Prince of Peace, to hear your story;
Help us resist the evil all around here;
May love abound here!

4. By your own Spirit, give your church a clear voice;
In this world's violence, help us make a new choice.
Help us to witness to the joy your peace brings,
Until your world sings![148]

Tune: HERZLIEBSTER JESU, 11.11.11.5

Within our darkest night you kindle the fire that never dies away. (*Brother Roger of Taizé)*[149]

16. RACIAL INJUSTICE

The United States occupies the land confiscated from Native Americans, and its economy was built on the backs of African slave labor. Integral to racial awakening is the admission of this genocide and cruelty, and the recognition that only when America acknowledges and repents of its original sins will this country truly flourish with genuine equality for all.

But let justice roll down like water and righteousness like an ever-flowing stream. *(Amos 5:24 NRSVue)*

PRAYERS

Dearest Jesus, come and sit with us today. Show us the lies that are still embedded in the soul of America's consciousness. Unmask the untruths we have made our best friends, for they seek our destruction and we are being destroyed, Lord. Reveal the ways the lies have distorted and destroyed our relationships. They break your shalom. . . . Jesus, give us courage to embrace the truth about ourselves and you and our world. Truth: we are all made in your image. Truth: you are God; we are not. You are God; money is not. You are God; jails, bombs, and bullets are not. And Jesus, give us faith to believe: redemption of people, relationships, communities, and whole nations is possible. Give us faith enough to renounce the lies and tear down the walls that separate us with our hands, with our feet, and with our votes! ***Amen.*** *(Lisa Sharon Harper)*[150]

God of justice, in your wisdom you create all people in your image, without exception. Through your goodness, open our eyes to see the dignity, beauty, and worth of every human being. Open our minds to understand that all your children are brothers and sisters in the same human family. Open our hearts to repent of racist attitudes, behaviors, and speech which demean others. Open our ears to hear the cries of those wounded by racial discrimination, and their passionate appeals for change. Strengthen our resolve to make amends for past injustices and to right the wrongs of history. And fill us with courage that we might seek to heal wounds, build bridges, forgive and be forgiven, and establish peace and equality for all in our communities. In Jesus' name we pray. ***Amen.*** *(Catholic Charities USA)*[151]

PSALM 13

How long, O Lord? Will you forget me forever?
 How long will you hide your face from me?

How long must I bear pain in my soul
 and have sorrow in my heart all day long?

How long shall my enemy be exalted over me?

Consider and answer me, O Lord my God!
 Give light to my eyes, or I will sleep the sleep of death,

and my enemy will say, "I have prevailed";
 my foes will rejoice because I am shaken.

But I trusted in your steadfast love;
 my heart shall rejoice in your salvation.

I will sing to the Lord,
 because he has dealt bountifully with me. (*NRSVue*)

SCRIPTURE ISAIAH 58:6–12

Is not this the fast that I choose:
 to loose the bonds of injustice,
 to undo the straps of the yoke,
to let the oppressed go free,
 and to break every yoke?
Is it not to share your bread with the hungry
 and bring the homeless poor into your house;

when you see the naked, to cover them,
  and not to hide yourself from your own kin?
Then your light shall break forth like the dawn,
  and your healing shall spring up quickly;
your vindicator shall go before you,
  the glory of the LORD shall be your rear guard.
Then you shall call, and the LORD will answer;
  you shall cry for help, and he will say, "Here I am."

If you remove the yoke from among you,
  the pointing of the finger, the speaking of evil,
if you offer your food to the hungry
  and satisfy the needs of the afflicted,
then your light shall rise in the darkness
  and your gloom be like the noonday.
The LORD will guide you continually
  and satisfy your needs in parched places
  and make your bones strong,
and you shall be like a watered garden,
  like a spring of water
  whose waters never fail.
Your ancient ruins shall be rebuilt;
  you shall raise up the foundations of many generations;
you shall be called the repairer of the breach,
  the restorer of streets to live in. (*NRSVue*)

LITANY ALFREDO JOSÉ GONÇALVES

Where do you come from; where are you going?

I come from all places; I have no name. I know pain and hunger. I seek land, home, food, life.

Where do you come from; where are you going?

I come from the underground, forgotten, dark, fetid and filthy. I seek dignity and peace, the day of light, citizenship.

Where do you come from; where are you going?

I come from the drainage ditch of abandonment. I know nostalgia and I lose hope. I seek gestures of friendship.

Where do you come from; where are you going?

I come from far and wide: black, yellow, white, indigenous. I am your "other," different. I am a person.

Where do you come from; where are you going?

I come from discrimination, from prejudice. I know walls, laws, fears, loneliness. I want a world without borders, or flags.

Where do you come from; where are you going?

I come from resistance, from the struggle, from a situation of senselessness; valiant and intrepid in the voyage of life. Of life I make rhyme and satire, on the way to the Great Homeland.[152]

REFLECTION MAHOGANY S. THOMAS

As a recent transplant to Washington, DC, I remember the summer of 2020 like it was yesterday. A church on fire. Broken glass. Shattered windows. Defaced property. Rubber bullets. Tear gas. Rage.

I was barely settled into my new home when protest for George Floyd and Breonna Taylor erupted not far away. In early June, less than twenty-four hours after a fire damaged the historic St. John's Episcopal Church, came the famous photo op: the 45th president of the United States used St. John's as a showcase for his imperial power. . . . A few months passed, and this is what we saw: Black Lives Matter banners on fire. Property destroyed. Hate crimes in front of churches. . . .

A few more weeks passed, and this is what we saw: the US Capitol in distress. Confederate flags and targeted hate. Mobs of angry people and, at the back of the crowd, banners that said, "Jesus Saves." As a nation, we witnessed religious rhetoric twisted into harmful actions, whiteness using god-talk as the vehicle to distort justice once again. This incident also transpired only a few miles from me; it felt personal. . . .

The common denominator in these disturbing moments is justice warped by white oppression, falsehoods knitted into our understandings of religion and embedded in our theologies. . . . Religion that was coopted under imperial whiteness and domination must repent and reemerge reimagined.

Without a willingness to reimagine our faith, we continue to wound those who are most vulnerable among us and hinder ourselves from healing. Without the determination to name the truth, we, too, distort justice. . . .

We have a responsibility to offer faith narratives that heal. To do that, we have to remove distortions and create new space for justice to emerge. . . . It is uncomfortable to think of ways we participate in stifling our neighbor's healing due to the very institutions we adore. It is not easy to think of the ways we have innocently contributed to one another's neglect. These tasks are not comfortable, and yet they are essential. Reimagining creates sustainable healing, not just for the individual but for our collective well-being. . . . Our sacred spaces do not have to be robed by imperial power or white oppression; they can become restorative again.[153]

Mahogany S. Thomas works in social justice and advocacy for marginalized communities. She moved to Washington, DC, after receiving her Master of Divinity from Yale Divinity School in 2020. She is now chief programming officer for the nonprofit Bread for the City, after having served as the executive minister of Washington, DC's Peoples Congregational United Church of Christ.

PRAYERS

O God, our gracious, heavenly Father, we thank Thee for the creative insights in the universe. We thank Thee for the lives of great saints and prophets in the past, who have revealed to us that we can stand up amid the problems and difficulties and trials of life and not give in. We thank Thee for our foreparents, who've given us something in the midst of the darkness of exploitation and oppression to keep going. And grant that we will go on with the proper faith and the proper determination of will, so that we will be able to make a creative contribution to this world and in our lives. In the name and spirit of Jesus we pray. ***Amen.*** *(Martin Luther King Jr.)*[154]

Great God of all people and nations: we give thanks for saints, martyrs, and leaders, throughout history and today, who have dedicated their lives to racial justice, equality for all people, and an end to racism and discrimination, and who stand with the neglected and weary. Pray that our actions, words, and service for the sake of our neighbor will be inspired and guided by the witness and example of these bold leaders. ***Amen.*** *(Evangelical Lutheran Church in America)*[155]

HYMN JAMES WELDON JOHNSON

1. Lift ev'ry voice and sing, till earth and heaven ring,
ring with the harmonies of liberty.
Let our rejoicing rise
high as the list'ning skies,
let it resound loud as the rolling sea.
Sing a song full of the faith that the dark past has taught us.
Sing a song full of the hope that the present has brought us.
Facing the rising sun
of our new day begun,
let us march on till victory is won.

2. Stony the road we trod,
bitter the chast'ning rod,
felt in the days when hope unborn had died;
yet with a steady beat,
have not our weary feet
come to the place for which our people sighed?
We have come over a way that with tears has been watered.
We have come, treading our path through the blood of the slaughtered,
out from the gloomy past,
till now we stand at last
where the bright gleam of our bright star is cast.

3. God of our weary years, God of our silent tears,
thou who hast brought us thus far on the way;
thou who hast by thy might
led us into the light,
keep us forever in the path, we pray,
lest our feet stray from the places, our God, where we met thee;
lest our hearts, drunk with the wine of the world, we forget thee;
shadowed beneath thy hand,
may we forever stand,
true to our God, true to our native land.[156]

Tune: LIFT EVERY VOICE AND SING, Irregular

Thus says the Lord: Stand at the crossroads and look, and ask for the ancient paths, where the good way lies; and walk in it, and find rest for your souls. *(Jeremiah 6:16 NRSVue)*

17. EDUCATION FOR EXTINCTION

Between the 1870s and the 1990s an estimated three hundred thousand Native children in Canada and the USA were forced to attend residential schools whose goal was to exterminate every aspect of Native culture and to reconstruct them as mainstream white Canadians and Americans. Hunger, starvation, disease, lack of medical care, beatings, and sexual abuse were common. The estimates are still coming in, but it is known that thousands and thousands of children died far from home in the most dire of circumstances.

And I heard a loud voice from the throne saying, "See, the home of God is among mortals. He will dwell with them; they will be his peoples, and God himself will be with them and be their God; he will wipe every tear from their eyes. Death will be no more; mourning and crying and pain will be no more, for the first things have passed away. . . . I will be their God and they will be my children. . . ." *(Revelation 21:3–4, 7b NRSVue)*

PRAYERS

Today we are invited to remember and lament. These little ones who died were not just Indigenous children belonging to someone else. They were part of *our* family, *our* children, *our* babies. So, let us lament together. And let us talk of how to go forward together. For this is not about *us* and *them*. We are all earth's children, created in the image and likeness of the Holy One. We can face the wrongs of our past, name them, and work toward building a future that holds up the dignity of all. May it be so. *(Helene Burns)*[157] Let us pray:

Into this sacred space we come in the knowledge that we as a people have not been our best selves and we have not always reflected the love of the Creator. We have been shaped and formed by the lives of those who have gone before us and we cry out in anguish for the wrongs that have been done in the name of the one we know to be love. Today we hold all of this in our beings, we sit with it, in hopes that Spirit will guide us into a better way and a new day. We give thanks for the courageous voices of our indigenous siblings who felt empowered to call us to account and who have had the grace to walk with us until we truly reflect Jesus' prayer that we all may be one. May Spirit be with us all. ***Amen.*** *(Valerie Kingsbury)*[158]

PSALM 124

If it had not been the Lord who was on our side
—let Israel now say—

if it had not been the Lord who was on our side,
when our enemies attacked us,

then they would have swallowed us up alive,
when their anger was kindled against us;

then the flood would have swept us away;
the torrent would have gone over us;

then over us would have gone
the raging waters.

Blessed be the Lord,
who has not given us
as prey to their teeth.

We have escaped like a bird
from the snare of the hunters;

the snare is broken,
and we have escaped.

Our help is in the name of the Lord,
who made heaven and earth. (*NRSVue*)

17. *Education for Extinction*

SCRIPTURE JEREMIAH 31:15–17 AND MATTHEW 2:16–18

Jeremiah 31:15–17

Thus says the LORD:
A voice is heard in Ramah,
    lamentation and bitter weeping.
Rachel is weeping for her children;
    she refuses to be comforted for her children,
    because they are no more.
Thus says the LORD:
Keep your voice from weeping
    and your eyes from tears;
for there is a reward for your work,
        says the LORD:
    they shall come back from the land of the enemy;
there is hope for your future,
        says the LORD:
    your children shall come back to their own country. (*NRSVue*)

Matthew 2:16–18

When Herod saw that he had been tricked by the magi, he was infuriated, and he sent and killed all the children in and around Bethlehem who were two years old or under, according to the time that he had learned from the magi. Then what had been spoken through the prophet Jeremiah was fulfilled:

"A voice was heard in Ramah,
    wailing and loud lamentation,
Rachel weeping for her children;
    she refused to be consoled, because they are no more." (*NRSVue*)

LITANY INSPIRED BY DOROTHY AND VINCE FONTAINE

Loving Creator, we pray for the little ones who were forcibly taken from their communities, homes, and families to live in residential schools.

Our hearts are broken.

In the quietness of our hearts we think of the children, some as young as three years old, who lost their lives and were buried in mass and unmarked graves, unbeknownst to those who loved them.

Our hearts are broken.

In the last moments of their lives, they faced death without their mother or father, without their siblings, grandparents, aunties, uncles, or friends.

Our hearts are broken.

Some of the survivors of the schools say that along with the pervasive sense of loneliness they felt in the absence of their families, they also endured abuse, trauma, hunger, shame, and fear.

Our hearts are broken.

We pray for an understanding of the powers and principalities, be they systemic or internal, which led us to such dark places, so that we can renounce them.

Lead us out of darkness into light.

Loving Creator, we also pray for the children's families and the other survivors who have wondered, for many years, about the fate of their schoolmates and loved ones.

Comfort everyone who grieves.

Instill in us your love, so that we can rightly love others; so that our prayers may become something more than empty words, clanging gongs, and broken promises.

May our journey towards reconciliation bear fruit and establish peace, equality, and justice in this land.

In this time of discovery and truth, may our prayers be answered and our voices heard. May our sacred fires burn strong, and may we be comforted and strengthened by your presence and fierce love.

Burn strong in us, sacred fires.[159]

17. Education for Extinction

REFLECTION ZITKALA-ŠA AND PAT WHITE HORSE-CARDA

It was night when we reached the school grounds. The lights from the windows of the large buildings fell upon some of the icicled trees that stood beneath them. We were led toward an open door, where the brightness of the lights within flooded out. . . . My body trembled more from fear than from the snow I trod upon. . . . I had arrived in the wonderful land of rosy skies, but I was not happy, as I had thought I should be. My long travel and the bewildering sights had exhausted me. I fell asleep, heaving deep, tired sobs. My tears were left to dry themselves in streaks, because neither my aunt nor my mother was near to wipe them away. . . .

I remember being dragged out, though I resisted by kicking and scratching wildly. In spite of myself, I was carried downstairs and tied fast in a chair.

I cried aloud, shaking my head all the while until I felt the cold blades of the scissors against my neck, and heard them gnaw off one of my thick braids. Then I lost my spirit. Since the day I was taken from my mother I had suffered extreme indignities. People had stared at me. I had been tossed about in the air like a wooden puppet. And now my long hair was shingled like a coward's! In my anguish I moaned for my mother, but no one came to comfort me. Not a soul reasoned quietly with me, as my own mother used to do; for now I was only one of many little animals driven by a herder. *(Zitkala-Ša)*[160]

Zitkala-Ša (1876–1938) was a Yankton Dakota political activist, writer, and musician whose publications include an account of her time at an Indiana boarding school from 1884 to 1887.

During the mid-twentieth century I attended St. Mary's Episcopal School for Indian Girls at Springfield, South Dakota. While I value this positive experience providing structure, caring teachers, and a variety of food and activities and where I made life lifelong friends, I also heard of the negative aspects of other boarding schools.

There were stories of the rigid discipline actions used by the staff to dole out punishment for violating rules. The most common report was of the nuns hitting the hands of the students with a wooden ruler. Many of these people shared they would never consider sending their children to a boarding school, even to this day. Their feelings of distrust and bitterness were evident from their facial expressions and tone of voice.

I did not consider sending my two sons to a boarding school because times change and I was able to provide for them at home with me. I would not want to separate them from me for any length of time. *(Pat White Horse-Carda)*[161]

Pat White Horse-Carda, an Episcopal priest, was born at Wagner, South Dakota, on the Yankton Sioux Reservation. She spent twenty-eight years as a public school educator and ten years in active service to four Mission churches.

PRAYERS

Ohiŋni wičhauŋkiksuyapi kte. We will always remember them. Dear Lord, Almighty God, we pray for all indigenous children who were in residential and boarding schools in Canada and the United States. Some died there; we ask that you give assurance to their descendants that their souls are with you and their ancestors. Some survived there; we ask that you give your healing grace to all who endured hardship while there and are still struggling with those memories. Lastly, we ask you to help us guard our children against harm in this world. All this we ask in the name of your son, Jesus Christ, who lives and reigns with you and the Holy Spirit, now and forever. ***Amen.*** *(Woniya Wakan [Holy Spirit] Episcopal Church)*[162]

Here I am, Lord. With this breath that you've given me, I lift my voice to you. As the deer pants for water so my soul longs for you. My whole being thirsts for you. You are my shelter and sustenance. You are the Word made flesh that dwells among us. I want to feast on your truth today. Come, fill me afresh. Let the wellspring of my heart pour out more of your goodness, your compassion, and your justice. ***Amen.*** *(Constance Padmore)*[163]

HYMN GRACIA GRINDAL

1. Let flow our tears in grief for this,
   our little ones, now gone from us,
   whom not so long ago were born,
   now all that's left to do is mourn,
   but we refuse to be consoled
   like Rachel weeping for her children.

2. Our voices join with all of those
who weep to hold their children close
but cannot reach beyond their dust
to lines they drew, their little trusts
and they refuse to be consoled
these parents weeping for their children.

3. All death and hope are met in one
born long ago who is God's Son
whose birth provoked the tyrant's rage
who tramples wanton through our age.
Still we refuse to be consoled
like Rachel weeping for her children.

4. For who of us can stop the hand
of brutal demons in the land
whose fury aims to hurt and kill
the innocents whose screams are still
upon the air and un-consoled,
with parents weeping for their children.

5. All we can do is turn to him
who died in old Jerusalem
and wept abandoned on the cross
disarming demons there for us
so one day we might be consoled
with Rachel weeping for our children.[164]

Tune: INNOCENTS, by Daniel Damon, 8.8.8.8.8.9.
Words © 2014 Hope Publishing

May the blessing of the God of Sarah and Abraham, the blessing of the Son, born of Mary, the blessing of the Holy Spirit, who watches over us as a mother watches over her children, be with us all. ***Amen.*** *(Lois Wilson)*[165]

18. CIVIL UNREST

We gather in city streets, town squares, and at our nation's capitol to call attention to just causes. We meet to celebrate, to demonstrate, and to unite in solidarity. Sharing and drawing strength from each other is part of our human experience. But without dialogue, prayer, and the desire for reconciliation, mass public demonstrations may tear down the very foundations of the society they aim to build.

"A house divided against itself cannot stand." (*Abraham Lincoln*)[166]

PRAYERS

Eternal God, in whose perfect kingdom no sword is drawn but the sword of righteousness, no strength known but the strength of love: so mightily spread abroad your Spirit that all people may be gathered under the banner of the Prince of Peace, as children of one God; to whom be honor and glory, now and forever. ***Amen.*** *(Episcopal Church)*[167]

O God of Miriam and Moses, and of all the prophets of justice and mercy in every religion and civil state, pour forth your Spirit upon us, that we have the courage to speak truth in a nation and world buzzing with propaganda; passion to seek peace in a nation and world addicted to violence; and strength to say "No" to all persons and authorities that exclude or defame any of your daughters and sons. Strengthen us to say "Yes" to all persons and authorities that welcome, heal, and honor all your children.

O God of Jesus and Mohammed, and of all the little creatures and children of this blue-green planet, you who side with no nation because you are the judge of all nations, you who call the rich and powerful to account because you care for the poor and vulnerable: feed us with the bread of your justice, fill us with the wine of your joy, that our hope may ever be nourished by your amazing grace. Surround us with sisters and brothers who will laugh and weep with us, picket and pray with us, that we may keep the faith, demonstrate hope, and love one another, no matter what. ***Amen.*** (*Robert Raines)*[168]

CANTICLE ECCLESIASTES 3:1–8

For everything there is a season and a time for every matter under heaven:

a time to be born and a time to die;

a time to plant and a time to pluck up what is planted;

a time to kill and a time to heal;

a time to break down and a time to build up;

a time to weep and a time to laugh;

a time to mourn and a time to dance;

a time to throw away stones and a time to gather stones together;

a time to embrace and a time to refrain from embracing;

a time to seek and a time to lose;

a time to keep and a time to throw away;

a time to tear and a time to sew;

a time to keep silent and a time to speak;

a time to love and a time to hate;

a time for war and a time for peace. (*NRSVue*)

SCRIPTURE ACTS 21:30–36

Then all the city was aroused, and the people rushed together. They seized Paul and dragged him out of the temple, and immediately the doors were shut. While they were trying to kill him, word came to the tribune of the cohort that all Jerusalem was in an uproar. Immediately he took soldiers and centurions and ran down to them. When they saw the tribune and the soldiers, they stopped beating Paul. Then the tribune came, arrested him, and ordered him to be bound with two chains; he inquired who he was and what he had done. Some in the crowd shouted one thing, some another; and as he could not learn the facts because of the uproar, he ordered him to be brought into the barracks. When Paul came to the steps, the violence of the mob was so great that he had to be carried by the soldiers. The crowd that followed kept shouting, "Away with him!" (*NRSVue*)

LITANY PETER J. SCAGNELLI

O God, author and giver of peace, in whose image and likeness each of us has been created with a human dignity worthy of respect on earth and destined for eternal glory,

Listen to the cry that rises from every corner of this fragile earth, from our human family torn by violent conflict:

Give peace in our time, O good and gracious God, that peace which, as your Son Jesus Christ told us and as we have experienced in these days,

is a peace which the world cannot give.

To world leaders grant the wisdom to see beyond the boundaries of race, religion, and nation to that common humanity that makes us all your children and brothers and sisters to one another.

To those who have taken up arms in anger or revenge or even in the cause of justice,

grant the grace of conversion to the path of peaceful dialogue and constructive collaboration.

To the innocent who live in the shadow of war and terror, especially the frightened children,

be a shelter and strength, their haven and hope.

And to those who have already lost their lives as victims of human cruelty,

open wide your arms and enfold them all in the embrace of your compassion, healing, and everlasting life.

Grant this through Jesus Christ, your Son, our Lord.[169]

REFLECTION POPE FRANCIS

We must regain the conviction that we need one another, that we have a shared responsibility for others and the world, and that being good and decent are worth it. We have had enough of immorality and the mockery of ethics, goodness, faith, and honesty. . . . When the foundations of social life are corroded, what ensues are battles over conflicting interests, new forms of violence and brutality, and obstacles to the growth of a genuine culture of care. . . .

Saint Therese of Lisieux invites us to practice the little way of love, not to miss out on a kind word, a smile, or any small gesture which sows peace and friendship. . . . Love, overflowing with small gestures of mutual care, is also civic and political, and it makes itself felt in every action that seeks to build a better world. Love for society and commitment to the common good are outstanding expressions of a charity which affects not only relationships between individuals but also . . . social, economic, and political ones. . . . Along with the importance of little everyday gestures, social love moves us to devise larger strategies to halt environmental degradation and to encourage a "culture of care" which permeates all of society.[170]

The papal encyclical, Laudato Sì, *from which this reflection is drawn, is Pope Francis's seminal treatise on care for earth and the interconnectedness of life in all its forms.*

PRAYERS

Almighty God, who has given us this good land for our heritage: We humbly beseech you that we may always prove ourselves a people mindful of your favor and glad to do your will. Bless our land with honorable industry, sound learning, and respect and appreciation for all citizens. Save us from violence, discord, and confusion; from pride and arrogance, and from every evil way. Defend our liberties, and fashion into one united people the multitudes . . . of many kindreds and tongues. Endue with the spirit of wisdom those to whom in your Name we entrust the authority of government, that there may be justice and peace at home, and that, through obedience to your law, we may show forth your praise among the nations of the earth. In the time of prosperity, fill our hearts with thankfulness, and in the day of trouble, suffer not our trust in you to fail; all of which we ask through Jesus Christ our Lord. ***Amen.*** *(Episcopal Church)*[171]

In the beginning you beamed light that shines in the darkest hour,
light that no darkness could overcome:
Pierce the soul of this nation with your light,
and enlighten everyone with your divine wisdom.
Pierce the soul of this nation with your light,
and blind the demons of violence and hate.
Pierce the soul of this nation with your light,
that our chests draw in hope
and our hands grasp with strength
and our innards gird with all their might
and our hearts pump the lifeblood
of an unlikely, luminous new beginning being born. ***Amen.***
(Anna E. Rossi)[172]

HYMN CAROLYN WINFREY GILLETTE

1. God of Love, we've known division and we've seen its awful cost.
We have struggled as a nation, and there's much that we have lost.
We have been a house divided—and, divided we can't stand.
May our nation be united; give us peace throughout this land.

2. Turn us, Lord, from what divides us—fear that drives us far apart,
greed that leads to great injustice, racist ways that break your heart.
May we seek what brings together—hearts that bear each other's pain,
care and mercy toward our neighbor, love that welcomes strangers in.

3. May we all, in conversation, speak the truth and listen well.
May we hear, across this nation, stories others have to tell.
May we learn from other cultures and be blessed by their worldview.
May we serve with one another—loving others, loving you.

4. You have challenged us to goodness; you have shown a kinder way.
It's your love that now inspires us as we seek a better day.
May we end our harsh division; may we stop the hate and fear.
Make us one, Lord, as a nation; may we be united here.[173]

Tune: BEACH SPRING, 8.7.8.7 D

Let us pray President Lincoln's immortal words of reconciliation and healing from his second inaugural address:

With malice toward none; with charity for all; with firmness in the right, as God gives us to see the right, let us strive on to finish the work we are in; to bind up the nation's wounds; . . . to do all that may achieve and cherish a just and a lasting peace, among ourselves, and with all nations. ***Amen.*** *(Abraham Lincoln)*[174]

19. WAR

The casualties of war are innocent victims who happen to be in the wrong place at the wrong time. They are the elderly, the weak, the disabled, the impoverished, and children who cannot evacuate; they are the soldiers fighting wars declared by old men who never see a battle field. War robs the poor and destroys the earth; war causes fear, terror, and disruption; war makes enemies of friends; it kills the future; in the aftermath it may lead to post-traumatic stress syndrome and suicide. War has no winners.

He shall judge between many peoples and shall arbitrate between strong nations far away; they shall beat their swords into plowshares and their spears into pruning hooks; nation shall not lift up sword against nation, neither shall they learn war any more . . . *(Micah 4:3 NRSVue)*

PRAYERS

God of the nations, whose sovereign rule brings justice and peace, have mercy on our broken and divided world. Shed abroad your peace in the hearts of all and banish from them the spirit that makes for war, that all races and peoples may learn to live as members of one family and in obedience to your law, through your Son, Jesus Christ, our Lord. ***Amen.*** *(Anglican Church of Australia)*[175]

Lord of all people and all nations, we lift before you (the people of __________), each girl and boy, each woman and man living in fear of what tomorrow might bring. We long for a time you spoke of through your prophet Isaiah, when weapons of war would be beaten into plowshares, when nation will no longer lift up sword against nation. We cry out to you for peace. Protect those who only desire and deserve to live in security and safety; comfort those who fear for their lives and the lives of their loved ones; change the hearts of those set on violence and aggression; fill leaders with great wisdom to find paths to peace. Please, Lord, come and have your way in your world, may your will be done here on earth as it is in heaven, may your peace reign, now and always. We lift this prayer to you, our God who is able to do more than we can ever ask or imagine, in the name of Christ our Savior. ***Amen.*** *(David Thomas)*[176]

PSALM 27:1–6A, 7, 9A, 11, 13–14

The LORD is my light and my salvation;
 whom shall I fear?

The LORD is the stronghold of my life;
 of whom shall I be afraid?

When evildoers assail me
 to devour my flesh—

my adversaries and foes—
 they shall stumble and fall.

Though an army encamp against me,
 my heart shall not fear;

though war rise up against me,
 yet I will be confident.

One thing I asked of the LORD;
 this I seek:

to live in the house of the LORD
 all the days of my life,

to behold the beauty of the LORD,
 and to inquire in his temple.

For he will hide me in his shelter
 in the day of trouble;

he will conceal me under the cover of his tent;
 he will set me high on a rock.

Now my head is lifted up
 above my enemies all around me. . . .

Hear, O LORD, when I cry aloud;
 be gracious to me and answer me! . . .

Do not hide your face from me.

Do not turn your servant away in anger,
 you who have been my help. . . .

Teach me your way, O LORD,
 and lead me on a level path
 because of my enemies. . . .

I believe that I shall see the goodness of the LORD
 in the land of the living.

Wait for the LORD;
 be strong, and let your heart take courage;
 wait for the LORD! (*NRSVue*)

SCRIPTURE LAMENTATIONS 5:1–5, 9–10, 13–17, 19–20

Remember, O LORD, what has befallen us;
 look, and see our disgrace!
Our inheritance has been turned over to strangers,
 our homes to aliens.
We have become orphans, fatherless;
 our mothers are like widows.
We must pay for the water we drink;
 the wood we get must be bought.
With a yoke on our necks we are hard driven;
 we are weary, we are given no rest. . . .
We get our bread at the peril of our lives,
 because of the sword in the wilderness.
Our skin is black as an oven
 from the scorching heat of famine. . . .

Young men are compelled to grind,
  and boys stagger under loads of wood.
The old men have left the city gate,
  the young men their music.
The joy of our hearts has ceased;
  our dancing has been turned to mourning.
The crown has fallen from our head;
  woe to us, for we have sinned!
Because of this our hearts are sick;
  because of these things our eyes have grown dim. . . .
But you, O Lord, reign forever;
  your throne endures to all generations.
Why have you forgotten us completely?
  Why have you forsaken us these many days? (*NRSVue*)

LITANY CREATION JUSTICE MINISTRIES

God, we come to you in grief and despair for the state of your creation.

Lord, have mercy on your planet and people.

Today, we look with an unflinching gaze at the tragedy of nations at war, and into the reality of climate catastrophe, because we are to be a people who do not turn away from suffering and injustice.

Lord, have mercy on your planet and people.

May our lament turn to compassion and our rage turn to action.

Lord, have mercy on your planet and people.

When hope seems foolish and impossible, may we continue to work for the restoration of this world.

Lord, have mercy on your planet and people.

In grief, despair, and lament, we offer this prayer through Jesus Christ, our Creator, Redeemer, and Sustainer.[177]

REFLECTION OLGA AIVAZOVSKA

At 5 am, on February 24, 2022, I woke up to the sounds of explosions around Kyiv. I had fifteen minutes to pack my belongings and leave my home. Now, when I fall asleep in other temporary places, I dream of my home, where I learned how to bake bread during lockdown last year. At such moments, I keep asking myself—what did I, what did we, do wrong? And then, I remember that my whole life, I've been fighting for the rights and freedoms that my beloved husband is defending right now on the frontline. We can't blame ourselves—we can only blame the aggressor state for this war. . . .

Mariupol was a beautiful, modern city on the coast. Roses lined every street. They should be blooming soon, filling the air with a charming fragrance. But the city was wiped off the face of the earth by Russians. Four hundred thousand civilians used to live there. The town was blocked and violently exterminated for weeks. . . .

So, close your eyes and think of the peaceful night in your home, in your cozy bed. You're warm and comfortable. My imagination today, though, can only evoke the horrible images of the cities, villages captured by Russians, or liberated, with their civilians executed. We will never be able to sleep again without those memories of the war.[178]

Olga Aivazovska, a forcibly displaced Ukrainian civil society leader, gave this account of her experience of the Russian invasion of Ukraine at the 14th Annual Geneva Summit for Human Rights and Democracy in 2022.

PRAYERS

O Lord, you love justice and you establish peace on earth. We bring before you the disunity of today's world; the absurd violence, and the many wars which are breaking the courage of the peoples of the world. Send your Spirit and renew the face of the earth; teach us to be compassionate towards the whole human family; strengthen the will of all those who fight for justice and for peace, and give us that peace which the world cannot give. ***Amen.*** *(Masamba ma Mpolo and Mengi Kilandamoko)*[179]

Eternal God, our only hope, our help in times of trouble: show nations ways to work out differences. Do not let threats multiply or power be used without compassion. May your will overrule human willfulness, so that people may agree and settle claims peacefully. Hold back those who are impulsive, lest their desire for vengeance overwhelm our common welfare. Bring peace to earth, through Jesus Christ, the Prince of Peace and Savior of us all. ***Amen.*** *(Presbyterian Church USA)*[180]

HYMN CONSTANCE CHERRY

1. When will people cease their fighting?
   When will armies wage no war,
   nations conquer not their neighbor,
   weapons idle, used no more?
   When will guns and bombs be silent?
   When will captives be set free?
   All creation groans in longing
   for the world's true liberty.

2. Floods and earthquakes, drought and famine
   plague the world with awesome ill,
   but far greater is war's horror
   caused by human, stubborn will.
   Blest are those who, working, praying,
   purpose in their hearts to be
   instruments of peace, committed
   to the nations' harmony.

3. As we strive for peace with vigor,
   hoping to be shown the way,
   we are strengthened in the knowledge
   of a future, perfect day;
   for we know that deeper, richer
   peace is ours when Christ shall reign:
   then will all our swords be plowshares
   and God's children free from pain.[181]

Tune: RUSTINGTON, 8.7.8.7 D. Words © 1990 Hope Publishing

Eternal Light, shine in our hearts;
Eternal Goodness, deliver us from evil;
Eternal Power, be our support;
Eternal Wisdom, scatter the darkness of our ignorance;

Eternal Compassion, have mercy upon us;
Through Jesus Christ our Lord. *(Alcuin)*[182]

20. REFUGEES

Refugees—people seeking refuge in countries other than where they were born—are forced out by poverty, war, and political unrest. The eighty-two million refugees worldwide, many of them children, have been forced to leave behind everything that they loved and cherished. When we welcome the stranger, the orphan, the naked, the widow, children, the hungry and thirsty, we welcome Jesus.

The LORD is near to the brokenhearted and saves the crushed in spirit. *(Psalm 34:18 NRSVue)*

PRAYERS

God made the dazzling heavens and abundant earth, the seas and all that is in them. God secures justice for the oppressed, the outcast, and those forced to journey to unknown lands. The Holy One lifts up those who are bowed down and watches over the stranger, the orphan, the widow, and the refugee. God weeps with those who weep and carries us all in a loving embrace. God's power is in all, under all, and over all. God will reign forever, to all generations. ***Amen.*** *(Anne Rowthorn)*[183]

Dear God of all humanity, be near us as we pray for all the uprooted people in the world, especially those who have fled their countries and have become refugees and those who have been forced to live like refugees in their own lands. Let us remember our friends and our sisters and brothers throughout the world: those whose rights have been violated; those who work hard and risk their lives that the rights of others may be respected;

those who have walked towards God's reign of justice, peace, and wholeness of life; and those who have been uprooted from their lands due to war, conflict, and the destruction of their environments. God, you made the heavens and the earth, there is no place you cannot reach; there is no journey that you have not traveled; there are no people beyond your care. You who are Spirit and Comforter, be with us now. ***Amen.*** *(Uniting Church in Australia and the Asian Church Conference)*[184]

PSALM 137:1–4

By the rivers of Babylon—
  there we sat down, and there we wept
  when we remembered Zion.

On the willows there
  we hung up our harps.

For there our captors
  asked us for songs,

and our tormentors asked for mirth, saying,
  "Sing us one of the songs of Zion!"

How could we sing the LORD's song
  in a foreign land? (*NRSVue*)

PSALM 143:1, 3, 9, 10B–11

Hear my prayer, O LORD;
  give ear to my supplications in your faithfulness;

answer me in your righteousness. . . .

For the enemy has pursued me,
  crushing my life to the ground,
  making me sit in darkness like those long dead. . . .

Save me, O LORD, from my enemies;
  I have fled to you for refuge. . . .

Let your good spirit lead me on a level path.

For your name's sake, O Lord, preserve my life.

In your righteousness bring me out of trouble. (*NRSVue*)

SCRIPTURE MATTHEW 2:13–23

Now after they had left, an angel of the Lord appeared to Joseph in a dream and said, "Get up, take the child and his mother, and flee to Egypt, and remain there until I tell you; for Herod is about to search for the child, to destroy him." Then Joseph got up, took the child and his mother by night, and went to Egypt and remained there until the death of Herod. This was to fulfill what had been spoken by the Lord through the prophet, "Out of Egypt I have called my son."

When Herod saw that he had been tricked by the magi, he was infuriated, and he sent and killed all the children in and around Bethlehem who were two years old or under, according to the time that he had learned from the magi. Then what had been spoken through the prophet Jeremiah was fulfilled:

"A voice was heard in Ramah,
  wailing and loud lamentation,
Rachel weeping for her children;
  she refused to be consoled, because they are no more."

When Herod died, an angel of the Lord suddenly appeared in a dream to Joseph in Egypt and said, "Get up, take the child and his mother, and go to the land of Israel, for those who were seeking the child's life are dead." Then Joseph got up, took the child and his mother, and went to the land of Israel. But when he heard that Archelaus was ruling Judea in place of his father Herod, he was afraid to go there. And after being warned in a dream, he went away to the district of Galilee. There he made his home in a town called Nazareth, so that what had been spoken through the prophets might be fulfilled, "He will be called a Nazarene." (*NRSVue*)

LITANY UNITING CHURCH IN AUSTRALIA AND ASIAN CHURCH CONFERENCE

As we face this day, O God, find those who are lost, separated from those they love, crossing unknown borders, without a country or home:

Find them, God, who always seeks for the lost, and cover them in safety as a hen covers her chickens.

As we face this day, O God, stand among those in refugee camps around the world, in the hunger of despair, in the crowds and the emptiness, in the wet and the thirstiness:

Be their hope and their strength in their crying out for justice, and open the ears of the world to hear their cries.

As they face this day, O God, may those who live with us, uprooted from their homelands, find a new home where their history is respected, their gifts and graces celebrated, and their fear lifted from them.

May we be their home, may we be the ones who open our hearts in welcome.

As we face this day, O God, sing to us your song of encouragement, paint for us your bright pictures of a new world where people need not flee from wars and oppression, where no one lacks a country or a home, and where we are all part of your new creation.

For we long to be your people, in spirit and in truth. We pray in the name of Jesus Christ, who knew the life of a refugee. *Amen.*[185]

REFLECTION ALLA RENÉE BOZARTH

I was nine years old.
My mother took me with her
to the train station to welcome
refugees from their war-torn
homeland.

There were parents with children.
There were grandparents.
They were smiling, but sad.
Each one carried one small bag
and the clothes on their backs.
Their homes were destroyed.

They spoke no English.
I was witnessing their birth

into their unknown future
in a foreign land.

They needed water and food.
They needed warm clothing
and blankets and a place to sleep.
They needed friends, and work,
and schools, and a way to learn
a new language. These things
would come. They were worlds away
from the friends and family and home
they loved and would never see again.

It was their first day out of the world
they had known and loved, destroyed.
Their first day out of their familiar heaven,
attacked, bombed, and turned into hell.

I offered them hope and a smile. All I had
I gave them. All I had was flowers.[186]

Alla Renée Bozarth is an Episcopal priest, poet, and the author of A Journey through Grief *and* Life Is Goodbye / Life Is Hello: Grieving Well through All Kinds of Loss. *She is well-acquainted with the refugee experience. Alla wrote of her gratitude for her mother's experience as a refugee from Russia, "Mama? Are you listening? Can you see this? Your daughter is alive because you fled your home to escape from soldiers with bayonets who had burned down the whole farmhouse and killed most of the men in your family, who had arrested the educated women and sent them to concentration camp gulags. . . ."*[187]

PRAYERS

Merciful God, we pray for all whose desperation leads them to the sea, to undertake perilous voyages, often following dangerous journeys over land: those escaping brutal wars, those fleeing religious persecution, those escaping climate disasters and economic ruin, those looking for hope in a hopeless situation. May we look beyond our own fears and concerns to the needs of those who have nothing, risk everything, and depend on the kindness of strangers. May our hearts be opened, our leaders challenged, and our self-interest reproached, in Jesus' name. ***Amen.*** (*Christian Aid UK*)[188]

O God, you have made us in your own image and redeemed us through Jesus Christ your Son. Look with compassion on the whole human family, take away the arrogance and hatred that infect our hearts, break down the walls that separate us, unite us in bonds of love, and, through our struggle and confusion, work to accomplish your purposes on earth; that, in your good time, all nations and races may serve you in harmony around your heavenly throne; through Jesus Christ our Lord. ***Amen.*** *(Presbyterian Church USA)*[189]

HYMN CAROLYN WINFREY GILLETTE

1. God, how can we comprehend—
Though we've seen them times before—
Lines of people without end
Fleeing danger, want, and war?
They seek safety anywhere,
Hoping for a welcome hand!
Can we know the pain they bear?
Help us, Lord, to understand!

2. You put music in their souls;
Now they struggle to survive.
You gave each one gifts and goals;
Now they flee to stay alive.
God of outcasts, may we see
How you value everyone,
For each homeless refugee
Is your daughter or your son.

3. Lord, your loving knows no bounds;
You have conquered death for all.
May we hear beyond our towns
To our distant neighbors' call.
Spirit, may our love increase;
May we reach to all your earth,
Till your whole world lives in peace;
Till we see each person's worth.[190]

Tune: ABERYSTWYTH, 7.7.7.7 D

20. Refugees

O Creator and Almighty God, you have promised strength for the weak, rest for the laborers, light for the way, grace for the trials, help from above, unfailing sympathy, undying love. O Creator and Almighty God, help us to live on in your promise. ***Amen***. *(Church of Pakistan)*[191]

21. EXTINCT AND ENDANGERED

Earth has endured five mass extinctions, the last one being sixty-six million years ago when 76 percent of all species disappeared. Earth may now be in the beginning stages of the Sixth Extinction. No one knows for sure the current rate of extinctions of plant and animal species, but there is widespread agreement that it is large. And many more plants and animals hover on the brink of extinction. Currently, endangered animal species include one in four mammals, one in four birds, a fifth of all reptiles, and one-third of all amphibians. About 30 percent of the world's species of trees are endangered. Truly, our earth is endangered.

Each year sees the disappearance of thousands of plant and animal species which we will never know, which our children will never see, because they have been lost for ever. The great majority become extinct for reasons related to human activity. Because of us, thousands of species will no longer give glory to God by their very existence, nor convey their message to us. We have no such right. *(Pope Francis)*[192]

PRAYERS

Great Giver of Life, we pause to remember our place at the beginning of the Sixth Great Extinction on Planet Earth. For 13.8 billion years creation has been groaning: bringing to birth, becoming more complex, more organized, more conscious. The other great extinctions during the past 450 million years happened by forces beyond anyone's control. Now, for the first time, our species is ruining whole ecosystems and aborting entire groups of interdependent species.

We acknowledge that we play a part in this dying by our carelessness, ignorance, and indifference. Forgive us our part in the death of healthy ecosystems and the resulting extinction of creatures in whom we believe divinity lives and acts. ***Amen.*** *(Terri MacKenzie, SHCJ)*[193]

What have we done, Lord? How did we not realize our impact? Whose voices did we fail to heed? Why did we let our greed take over? Where are people suffering today? Fires destroying towns amidst parched forests; hurricanes fueled by warm ocean waters; smog-trapped cities; rising sea levels; global temperatures breaking records; politicians floundering; decisions delayed; deadlines coming and going; and the echo of your voice to be stewards responsible for it all does not go away. What can we do, Lord? ***Amen.*** *(Spill the Beans)*[194]

PSALM 85:6–13

Will you not revive us again,
  so that your people may rejoice in you?

Show us your steadfast love, O Lord,
  and grant us your salvation.

Let me hear what God the Lord will speak,

for he will speak peace to his people,
to his faithful, to those who turn to him in their hearts.

Surely his salvation is at hand for those who fear him,
  that his glory may dwell in our land.

Steadfast love and faithfulness will meet;
  righteousness and peace will kiss each other.

Faithfulness will spring up from the ground,
  and righteousness will look down from the sky.

The Lord will give what is good,
  and our land will yield its increase.

Righteousness will go before him
and will make a path for his steps. (*NRSVue*)

SCRIPTURE ISAIAH 24:1–3 AND JEREMIAH 29:11–14

Isaiah 24:1–3

Now the Lord is about to lay waste the earth and make it desolate,
and he will twist its surface and scatter its inhabitants.
And it shall be, as with the people, so with the priest;
as with the male slave, so with his master;
as with the female slave, so with her mistress;
as with the buyer, so with the seller;
as with the lender, so with the borrower;
as with the creditor, so with the debtor.
The earth shall be utterly laid waste and utterly despoiled;
for the Lord has spoken this word. (*NRSVue*)

Silence.

Jeremiah 29:11–14

For surely I know the plans I have for you, says the Lord, plans for your welfare and not for harm, to give you a future with hope. Then when you call upon me and come and pray to me, I will hear you. When you search for me, you will find me; if you seek me with all your heart, I will let you find me, says the Lord, and I will restore your fortunes and gather you from all the nations and all the places where I have driven you, says the Lord, and I will bring you back to the place from which I sent you into exile. (*NRSVue*)

LITANY ANNE AND JEFFERY ROWTHORN

Eternal God, author of all, guardian and protector of all: we bring before you the multitude of our sorrows and our grief for the loss of our extinct sister and brother species.

Silence.

We remember—the Sicilian wolf, Japanese sea lion, bulbal antelope, Tasmanian tiger, golden toad, Caspian tiger, St. Helena darter, Guam flying fox, Pinta Island tortoise, Barbados racer snake, Christmas Island whiptale skink, Cuban macaw, Cuban coney, Galapagos giant rat, big-eared hopping mouse, New South Wales bandicoot, Saint Lucia giant rice rat, Darwin's Galapagos mouse, Hispaniola monkey, Nelson's rice rat, Anthony's wood rat, crescent nail-tail wallaby—they are gone; we grieve their loss.

We grieve. *Silence.*

We remember—the paradise parrot, dodo, passenger pigeon, great awk, Bachman's warbler, Carolina parakeet, Labrador duck, moa, Hawaiian mamo, laughing owl, heath hen, Seychelles parakeet, Norfolk duck, Marianne white-eye, Coturnix, Eskimo curlew, Lyall's wren, New Zealand quail, elephant bird, Kangaroo Island emu—they are gone; we grieve their loss.

We grieve. *Silence.*

We remember—the Jamaican giant galliwasp, Round Island burrowing boa, Yunnan newt, Rodrigues giant tortoise, Cape Verde giant skink, kawekaweau, Martinique giant ameiva, horned turtle, wonambi, giant monitor lizard, quinka—they are gone; we grieve their loss.

We grieve. *Silence.*

We raise our voices in prayer for all endangered animals and birds: among them the Siberian tiger, Bengal tiger, Malayan tiger, black rhino, whooping crane, Asian elephant, African elephant, wallaby, northern wombat, Arctic fox, mountain caribou, Saharan cheetah, African wild dog, North African ostrich, snow leopard, Alexander Archipelago wolf, red wolf, mountain gorilla, Borneo orangutan, golden lion tamarin, Australian koala, giant panda, dama gazelle—

Come quickly, O Holy God of the universe. Save them.

We pray for all endangered fish and other marine creatures; a few of them we name now: Atlantic bluefin tuna, North Atlantic right whale, hawksbill turtle, Galapagos penguin, short-tailed albatross, Hector's dolphin, whale shark, blue whale, sea otter, Steller sea lion, Cook Inlet beluga whale, Chinese sturgeon, Hawaiian monk seal, Amazonian manatee, winter skate, European eel, red hand fish, Nassau grouper, deep sea perch, Southern bluefin tuna, great sturgeon, Atlantic halibut—

Come quickly, O Holy God of the universe. Save them.

We pray for all endangered trees, among them: Monkey puzzle, Pacific yew, pan Brazil, big leaf mahogany, bristlecone pine, African boabab, African blackwood, Florida yew, giant sequoia, coastal redwood, Santa Cruz cypress, longleaf pine, Fraser fir, St. Helena gumwood, Honduras rosewood, dragon tree, Clan William cedar, Hawaiian loulu, the American chestnut, the American elm tree, St. Helena olive tree—

Come quickly, O Holy God of the universe. Save them.

We pray for bats and bees, salamanders, polar bears, butterflies, and all other plants and animals and insects that are close to extinction—

Come quickly, O Holy God of the universe, save them and awaken our minds and hearts to ensure that every living being has a chance to live and to prosper.[195]

REFLECTION J. DREW LANHAM

The Anthropocene is officially grounded. . . .

Three billion birds gone in the last fifty years. Intending no disrespect to ostriches, rheas, emus, cassowaries, kiwis, Guam rails, kakapos, penguins, and the rest of the flightless avians—this current predicament is Rachel's worse nightmare dropped dead as a pesticide-poisoned rain crow from the tree. . . .

What does "billions" mean exactly? I see grains of sand on a square foot of beach, or blades of grass on a prairie. The stars or particles of dust we come from, the number of miles and years distant just now reaching us as light from lamps that no longer exist.

Light that once even shone on the backs and rosy breasts of passenger pigeons, on the cypress green backs of Carolina parakeets. Light that once shone on heath hens, on big-beaked dodos, on great auks, on clam-eating Labrador ducks, on ivory-billed woodpeckers worthy of Lord God status. Light that shone on Bachman's warblers, dusky seaside sparrows, Eskimo curlews, and birds no one ever saw or even had the chance to name after some genocidal racist, faded into oblivion within a few measly human generations. For all these birds, we made the way to gone-ness simple. We plowed under, cut down, paved over, warmed up, sprayed out, and burned down everything we could. . . .

The billions aren't conceptual or modeled or opined in labs somewhere. They are a palpable loss, an absence of plumage, of song and of calls. Every bird I see, whether the allegedly common northern cardinal or the "list-worthy" olive-sided flycatcher at the top of the neighbors' dying maple tree, is worship worthy. . . . I know what the silence of a May morning portends. I know what the quiet sky minus migrating thrush on a full-mooned October night portends. I know what the shoreline with only a few red knots to untangle from the mixed flock of shorebirds portends. Grounded. Wings clipped. Skies emptied. I can feel the heaviness of them draining, can feel what Daedalus must have felt as he watched his son. That the fall was inevitable. The plunge predictable. And that it was avoidable.[196]

J. Drew Lanham is a poet, essayist, and wildlife biologist who teaches at Clemson University. He is a birder and conservationist and an award-winning writer of the book The Home Place: Memoirs of a Colored Man's Love Affair with Nature. *This reflection is from an article published in* Orion Magazine.

PRAYERS

Great Giver of Life, we come from, and we dwell in, the magnificent world in which you live and act. Our species is causing extinctions; our species can prevent them. Let us not be thwarted by the immensity of the challenge, for the Power working within us can do more than we can imagine. May the flame of God's love ever burn in our hearts, reminding us to help our threatened relatives. Enlighten us to find you in all creation; empower us to treat it accordingly; through Jesus Christ, whose respect for earth inspires us to live as he did. ***Amen.*** *(Terri MacKenzie, SHCJ)*[197]

Body of God, splendor of the Divine, in a world diminished, we are diminished. Wake us up, contain us, infuse us with a new belonging, expand our narrow vision, deliver us again by your life-giving grace. Encourage us as we lay down our arms, for only in your commonwealth is there life. May your Good Spirit re-enchant us, let everything be held sacred again, re-found us in your kingdom of simplicity and love. ***Amen.*** *(Peter Healy)*[198]

HYMN ANDREW PRATT

1. The care of our planet, the threat of extinction,
alerts us to need to be stewards of earth:
this place of great beauty, our God-given tenure,
the place of our nurture, the globe of our birth.

2. This place we must guard for each new generation,
to leave as we found it or, better, restored;
to share each resource without greed or pretension,
not barring the needy, not plunder, nor hoard.

3. The banquet of God is for all of God's people,
communion companions are both rich and poor,
our ultimate end will remove all distinctions,
no birthright or creed can obstruct heaven's door.

4. God's commonwealth love can encompass all nations,
but here in this place we must all make a start:
a life of acceptance of sister and brother,
the practice of loving, a God-given art.[199]

Tune: STREETS OF LAREDO, 12.11.12.11. Words

I have set before you life and death, blessings and curses. Choose life so that you and your descendants may live . . . so that you may live long in the land that the LORD swore to give to your ancestors, to Sarah and Abraham, to Rebecca and Isaac, to Leah and Rachel and Jacob. *(Inspired by Deuteronomy 30:19–20)*

22. CLIMATE CRISIS

Within the next twenty years 90 percent of the world's population will be affected by at least one or more major climate risks.[200] *They are already making climate nomads of people fleeing fires, floods, rising seas, and excessive heat. The climate crisis is threatening agriculture, fresh water supplies, jobs, and the economy, to say nothing of the harm done to plants and animals of earth, sky, and sea. "Whether humanity has the collective wisdom to navigate the Anthropocene to sustain a livable biosphere for people and civilizations, as well as for the rest of life with which we share the planet, is the most formidable challenge facing humanity."*[201]

Ultimately, the decision to save the environment must come from the human heart. The key point is a call for a genuine sense of universal responsibility that is based on love, compassion, and clear awareness. (*The Dalai Lama)*[202]

PRAYERS

Let us give thanks for the world around us. Thanks for all the creatures, stones, and plants. Let us learn their lessons and seek their truths, so that their path might be ours, and we might live in harmony, a better life. May the earth continue to live. May the heavens above continue to live. May the rains continue to dampen the land. May the wet forests continue to grow, then the flowers shall bloom and we people shall live again. ***Amen***. *(Attributed to Hawaiian indigenous tradition)*[203]

Blessed are you, God of the universe. You have created us and given us life. Blessed are you, God of the planet earth. You have set our world like a radiant jewel in the heavens and filled it with action, beauty, suffering, struggle, and hope. Blessed are you, God of every land, in all your people who live here, in all lessons we have learned, in all that remains to be done. Blessed are you because you need us; because you make us worthwhile; because you give us people to love and work to do in your universe, for your world and for ourselves. ***Amen.*** *(The Church of the Province of New Zealand)*[204]

PSALM 46:1–7, 10–11

God is our refuge and strength,
a very present help in trouble.

Therefore we will not fear, though the earth should change,
though the mountains shake in the heart of the sea;

though its waters roar and foam,
though the mountains tremble with its tumult. . . .

There is a river whose streams make glad the city of God,
the holy habitation of the Most High.

God is in the midst of the city; it shall not be moved;
God will help it when the morning dawns.

The nations are in an uproar, the kingdoms totter;
he utters his voice; the earth melts.

The Lord of hosts is with us;
the God of Jacob is our refuge. . . .

"Be still, and know that I am God!
I am exalted among the nations;
I am exalted in the earth."

The Lord of hosts is with us;
the God of Jacob is our refuge. (*NRSVue*)

SCRIPTURE ISAIAH 24:4–13

The earth dries up and withers;
  the world languishes and withers;
  the heavens languish together with the earth.
The earth lies polluted
  under its inhabitants,
for they have transgressed laws,
  violated the statutes,
  broken the everlasting covenant.
Therefore, a curse devours the earth,
  and its inhabitants suffer for their guilt;
therefore, the inhabitants of the earth dwindled,
  and few people are left.
The wine dries up,
  the vine languishes,
  all the merry-hearted sigh.
The mirth of the timbrels is stilled;
  the noise of the jubilant has ceased;
  the mirth of the lyre is stilled.
No longer do they drink wine with singing;
  strong drink is bitter to those who drink it.
The city of chaos is broken down;
  every house is shut up so that no one can enter.
There is an outcry in the streets . . . ;
  all joy has reached its eventide;
  the gladness of the earth is banished.
Desolation is left in the city;
  the gates are battered into ruins.
For thus it shall be on the earth
  and among the nations,
as when an olive tree is beaten,
  as at the gleaning when the grape harvest is ended. (*NRSVue*)

LITANY JANE DEREN

We pray for the waters of the world, that they may be restored to health and filled with bountiful life.

God of Creation, help us to respect and renew the earth.

We pray for the earth's soil, that its richness be protected to ensure abundant harvests for all.

God of Creation, help us to respect and renew the earth.

We pray for all creatures who share earth with us, that their beauty and diversity will be preserved.

God of Creation, help us to respect and renew the earth.

We pray for our brothers and sisters around the world who have been and will be directly impacted by the effects of climate change.

God of Creation, help us to respect and renew the earth.

We pray for future generations, may they learn from our environmental irresponsibility, and be good stewards living simply and in harmony with all your creation.

God of Creation, help us to respect and renew the earth.

We pray for all human beings, that we will be filled with a spirit of concern for the future of our environment; bring an end to the exploitation of the earth's scarce resources, and live as responsible stewards protecting and respecting this gift of creation God has placed in our hands.

God of Creation, help us to respect and renew the earth.

We pray for wisdom for decision makers around the world, that wealthy nations may make amends for the harm they have done to the environment and find creative and just solutions to protect all of creation and ensure climate justice.

God of Creation, help us to respect and renew the earth.[205]

REFLECTION GRETA THUNBERG

I'm inviting you to be part of the solution. . . .

Five years ago world leaders signed the Paris Agreement and they promised to keep the global average temperature rise to well below 2 degrees Celsius and to pursue 1.5 degrees to safeguard future living conditions. Since then, a lot has happened but the action needed is still nowhere in sight. The gap between what we need to do and what is actually being done is widening by the minute. We are still speeding in the wrong direction.

The five years following the Paris Agreement have been the five hottest years ever recorded and during that time the world has also emitted more than 200 gigatons of CO_2. Commitments are being made, distant hypothetical targets are being set, and big speeches are being given, yet when it comes to the immediate action we need, we're still in a state of complete denial. . . . If you read through the current best available science, you realize that the climate crisis and the ecological crisis cannot be solved without systems change. That's no longer an opinion. That's a fact. The climate crisis is only part of a bigger sustainability crisis. For too long we have been distancing ourselves from nature, mistreating the planet, our only home; living as if there was no tomorrow. At the current emissions rate, our remaining CO_2 budgets . . . will be completely gone within seven years, long before we'll even have a chance to deliver on our 2030 and 2050 targets.

But I am telling you there is hope because the people have not yet been made aware. We cannot solve a crisis without treating it as a crisis, nor can we treat something like a crisis unless we understand the emergency. So let's make this our main priority; let's unite and spread awareness. Then we can act; then change will come. This is the solution. We are the hope. We are the people.[206]

At the age of fifteen, the Swedish climate activist Greta Thunberg began skipping school in order to stand in front of the Swedish Parliament every day holding a sign reading "School Strike for Climate" to bring urgent attention to the worldwide climate crisis. Following her example, student strikes began to appear around the globe. Thunberg has addressed the United Nations and international political meetings with her straightforward, direct, often chastising message on the need for action.

PRAYERS

Lord God, we thank you for the gift of life. We thank and praise you for the mystery of creation. We know that you are in us, and we in you. Guide us, therefore, in our efforts to hand on the earth to future generations, so that others can seek to understand your will and purpose in the world. Bring your love to perfection and magnify your holy name.

Help us overcome godlessness with love. Help us to support and protect the victims of climate change everywhere, especially those who've lost their homes or livelihoods to the ravages of famine, fire, and flood. Teach us to live in peace and harmony with all creation. Lord, in your name, ***Amen.*** *(Caritas, Australia)*[207]

Turn us around, O God. Turn us toward directions of care for your earth. Help us to desire the good of all your children and their welfare. May we adopt new practices and ways of using resources so the earth will be cared for through future years. Help us find ways to honor, sustain, and protect the earth so all people may share in its resources in health and safety and peace. Grant that we may restore the habitat you have given us, O God. Move us into new ways of care for creation and for all who inhabit the earth, our home. Bless the efforts of all who yearn for the fullness of your goodness and care to cover the earth. Move us by your Spirit to be at one with your creation and to seek bountiful lives for all.

Let all God's people say: ***Amen.*** *(Don McKim)*[208]

HYMN MARY LOUISE BRINGLE

1. Can you feel the seasons turning,
winds and waves grown wild and strange?
Can you feel creation groaning,
fearful of the coming change:
  ice caps melting, oceans rising,
  homes and habitations lost?
Can you feel the seasons turning?
Can you count the bitter cost?

2. Can you hear the creatures crying—
lynx and otter, wolf and whale?
Can you hear the Spirit sighing
as her children grieve and fail?
  Nature's poor, the first to suffer,
  pay the price of human greed.
Can you hear the creatures crying,
begging us to stop and heed?

3. Can you feel the seasons turning?
Storm clouds gather in the skies.
All around us, signs of warning
bid us open frightened eyes.
    Called by God to serve as stewards,
    till earth's garden greens and thrives,
can we learn in time to listen?
Can we turn and change our lives?[209]

Tune: EBENEZER, 8.7.8.7 D

May the grace of God, deeper than our imagination; the strength of Christ, stronger than our need; the communion of the Holy Spirit richer than our togetherness: guide and sustain us today and in all our tomorrows. ***Amen.*** (*Roger D. Knight*)[210]

23. LAMENT AND HOPE

We linger in lament; we neither hide from it, nor gloss over or deny it. It enters deeply into our souls. Lament evokes our tears, pierces our hearts and changes them. We offer our laments to God; we rest on the everlasting arms . . . and finally we move on in hope, knowing that ultimately all things work together to the glory of God.

Jerusalem, Jerusalem, the city that kills the prophets and stones those who are sent to it! How often have I desired to gather your children together as a hen gathers her brood under her wings . . . *(Matthew 23:37 NRSVue)*

PRAYER

Praise to you, holy God of the universe. You were there at the dawning of creation and you hold all things together. You roll out the ever-expanding celestial tapestry of bright stars, bursting supernovas, spinning planets, and galaxies beyond galaxies, yet you are as near to us as the air we breathe. You hover close to the newborn and you will soothe our dying breath. We open our hearts to you, to the earth and sky, to oceans and all that lives in them. All praise to you, holy God, author of all, who is in all and loves all. ***Amen.***
(Anne and Jeffery Rowthorn)[211]

PSALM 33:12–15, 18–22

Happy is the nation whose God is Yhwh!
Happy the people you choose as your own inheritance!

From the heavens you look forth, YHWH,
and see all of humankind.

From your dwelling place you watch
over all the peoples of the earth.

You shape the hearts of them all
and consider all their deeds. . . .

The eyes of YHWH look on those who stand in reverence,
on those who hope in God's love

to rescue them from death,
or to keep them alive during famine.

And so we wait for YHWH,
our help and our shield.

For in you our hearts find joy;
we trust in your holy name.

May your love be upon us, YHWH,
as we place our hope in you.[212]

SCRIPTURE ISAIAH 40:1–5, 28–31

Comfort, O comfort my people,
says your God.
Speak tenderly to Jerusalem,
and cry to her
that she has served her term,
that her penalty is paid,
that she has received from the LORD's hand
double for all her sins.

A voice cries out:
"In the wilderness prepare the way of the LORD;
make straight in the desert a highway for our God.
Every valley shall be lifted up,
and every mountain and hill be made low;
the uneven ground shall become level,
and the rough places a plain.

Then the glory of the LORD shall be revealed,
and all flesh shall see it together,
for the mouth of the LORD has spoken." . . .

Have you not known? Have you not heard?
The LORD is the everlasting God,
the Creator of the ends of the earth.
He does not faint or grow weary;
his understanding is unsearchable.
He gives power to the faint
and strengthens the powerless.
Even youths will faint and be weary,
and the young will fall exhausted,
but those who wait for the LORD shall renew their strength;
they shall mount up with wings like eagles;
they shall run and not be weary;
they shall walk and not faint. (*NRSVue*)

LITANY ANNE AND JEFFERY ROWTHORN

Holy God of creation; God of a thousand names, faces, and places; God at the beginning of time; God who created the stars and spun the planets: God, you have always been with us and with all that lives and moves in creation. We lament that we have not honored you and your precious earth.

Holy God of creation, we lament.

Through ignorance, greed, and indifference, we have poisoned the air, overheated the planet, despoiled the waters. Species are endangered and going extinct; thousands have been forced to move to higher ground and lower livable temperatures.

Holy God of creation, we lament.

Wars and conflicts, ancient grudges and taboos, guns and civil unrest are dividing your people.

Holy God of creation, we lament.

Even the ground beneath our feet cries out to you as trees of the forest are wantonly cut down and wildfires consume the land.

Holy God of creation, we lament.

Holy God of creation: we pray that you will open up our hearts and minds that we may see earth and all its systems, artifacts, and creatures with your eyes and heart and mind. Teach us to have hope.

To have hope—

is to believe that we can be open to the dream of God for a more loving world where all God's children of every race, land and culture are loved and adored.

To have hope—

is to honor all animals and creatures as God's own precious children.

To have hope—

is to feel the beauty in all of God's hills and mountains, valleys and dry places, and to protect them with our lives.

To have hope—

is to honor the sacred waters of earth and keep them plain and pure.

To have hope—

is to open our hearts to the poor, the refugee, the stranger, the despairing, and offer them help, hospitality, and jobs.

To have hope—

is to turn our prayers into action and to work for all that is good, and true and just.

To have hope—

is to become our best selves and build up the desolate places, and to make our homes and communities havens of love, joy, and peace.

To have hope—

is to begin again and again as many times as necessary until every dream of God is no longer a dream but reality.[213]

REFLECTION CATHERINE DE VINCK

I bow to the North and to the South
to the East and to the West.
I bow to the sky enameled blue
and to the wind-blown traveling clouds.
I bow to the ancestors:
women tracking the bison's herd,
men building shelters, making fires.
I bow to the children, born and unborn
holding the future hidden in their genes.
I bow to the animals, to the fox trotting in the woods.
I bow to the lion and the whale as well as to the snail
housed in its porcelain shell.
I bow to the light ascending every morning.
I bow to the night, to its dark portals.
I bow to the pale moon ever at work
pulling the tides, mirroring the sun.
I bow to the rain dripping from the roof
feeding streams released to the sea.
I bow to the stars, to their fiery tremors
held in the immense vastness of space.
I bow to the plants and trees, to the berries and apples.
I bow to all that is open and welcoming:
the calix of flowers, the heart of lovers.
I bow to all my years, past and present.
I bow to death waiting at the corner
ready to take me to new ways of being,
to larger territories of exploration.
I bow to the one we call God
unknown to us yet present here and now
in everything we see and feel and touch.
I bow to life in all its histories and shapes.
I bow forever in thanksgiving and love.[214]

Belgian by birth, Catherine de Vinck and her husband, José, came to the USA in 1948 and settled in New Jersey, where they raised a large family. One of their children, Oliver, was born with serious handicaps. He was blind and deaf; he could neither raise himself from his bed nor feed himself. For the next thirty-two years, Catherine and her whole family lovingly cared for Oliver, and Oliver had a profound effect on this extraordinary family. Throughout the years Catherine wrote magnificent hope-filled poetry. At her ninety-ninth birthday on February 22, 2021, she wrote the poem presented here as a reflection.

PRAYERS

All humankind is one vast family,
this world, our home.
We sleep beneath one roof, the starry sky.
We warm ourselves before one hearth, the blazing sun.
Upon one soil we stand, and breathe one air and drink one water and walk the night beneath one luminescent moon.
The children of the universe are we, family of one blood,
members in one worldwide family, this earth, our home.

All humankind is one vast family,
this world, our home.
We acknowledge the damage to our roof, the starry sky.
We recognize the rising heat which harms our seas, our plains, our forests, and the life therein. We lament the painful consequences of our choices on the sacred soil and air and water.
The children of the universe are we, family of one blood,
who bear responsibility for the hurt we cause each other and this earth, our home.

All humankind is one vast family,
this world, our home.
We pledge our care to all the life beneath one roof, the starry sky.
We honor all who seek the warmth of the blazing sun.
We will remember that upon one soil we stand, and breathe one air, and drink one water, and walk the night beneath one luminescent moon.
All children of the universe are we—creatures of the land and sea and air, all life that lives upon and within, this earth, our home. ***Amen.*** *(Adapted from the Book of Remembrance of the Cathedral of St. Paul the Apostle, Los Angeles)*[215]

Holy God, holy and mighty, holy immortal one, spirit of truth and justice, you are present at all times and in all places, filling all things: come now and abide with us. Search our hearts and minds; awaken our imaginations and lead us to compassionate action, in the name of Jesus Christ, who hears all our prayers. ***Amen.*** (*Anne and Jeffery Rowthorn)*[216]

HYMN ANDREW PRATT

1. A God of surprises beyond expectation,
   can capture our senses and brighten our night;
   for just when our hopes were contracting and fading
   the bridegroom arrives and our darkness is light.

2. Like bridesmaids still waiting to honor that bridegroom,
   our patience is waning and sleep clouds our eyes,
   but just before dawn when our minds least expect it,
   God enters the drama affirming the wise.

3. So are we awake to the hope and the wonder,
   amazed by the glory of sunlight and star,
   the promise of God in the midst of our turmoil,
   not somewhere far distant, but here where we are?[217]

Tune: KREMSER, 12.11.12.11. Words © 2011
Stainer & Bell, Ltd. (admin. Hope Publishing)

May God bless you with *discontent* with easy answers, half truths, and superficial relationships, so that you will live from deep within your heart.

May God bless you with *anger* at injustice, oppression, abuse, and exploitation of people, so that you will work for justice, equality, and peace.

May God bless you with *tears* to shed for those who suffer from pain, rejection, starvation, and war, so that you will reach out your hand to comfort them and to change their pain to joy.

May God bless you with the *foolishness* to think you can make a difference in this world, so that you will do the things which others tell you cannot be done.

If you have the courage to accept these blessings, then God will also bless you with:

happiness—because you will know that you have made life better for others.

inner peace—because you will have worked to secure an outer peace for others.

laughter—because your heart will be light.

faithful friends—because they will recognize your worth as a person.

These blessings are yours—not for the asking, but for the giving—from One who wants to be your companion, our God, who lives and reigns forever and ever. ***Amen.*** *(Ruth Fox, OSB)*[218]

EUCHARISTIC PRAYERS

Any of these liturgies may conclude as follows with a celebration of the Eucharist:

Following the prayers of confession and intercession, bread and wine are offered at the altar, prayed over, and shared according to the normal practice of the particular congregation.

Three Eucharistic prayers are given here for optional use in the celebration of the Sacrament.

The service then ends with the hymn.

EUCHARISTIC PRAYER I

The Lord be with you.

And also with you.

Lift up your hearts.

We lift them up to the Lord.

Let us give thanks to the Lord our God.

It is right to give our thanks and praise.

Blessed are you, gracious God,
Creator of light, Giver of life, Source of love.
You guide the sun, cradle the moon, and toss the stars.
At your word the earth was made
and spun on its course among the planets.
You breathe life into us
and set us among all your creatures,
in a covenant of love and service.
Even when we turn away from you, you do not forsake us.
You send your prophets to proclaim your justice,
to remind us of your promise of peace,
and to call us back to you.

Creator, Christ, and Spirit,
we praise you for your love revealed to us in Jesus,
who walks with us, our Wisdom and our Way,
sharing our joy and sorrow,
healing the sick,
feeding the hungry,
and setting the captives free.

So it is that we join the song of all creation
to proclaim your goodness:

Holy, holy, holy Lord,
God of power and might,
heaven and earth are full of your glory.
Hosanna in the highest.
Blessed is he who comes in the name of the Lord.
Hosanna in the highest.

Mighty and tender God, in Jesus of Nazareth
we recognize the fullness of your grace:
light, life, and love revealed
in words that confront and comfort us,
in teachings that challenge and change us,
in compassion that heals and frees us.

And now we gather at this table to remember
and to be filled with such longing for your realm
that we may rise together
to turn our worship into witness
and to follow in your way.

We remember that when Jesus ate with his friends,
he took a loaf of bread and, after blessing it,
he broke it and gave it to them, saying:
"Take, eat. This is my body given for you.
Each time you do this, remember me."
Then he took the cup and, after giving thanks,
passed it to his friends, saying:
"Drink. This cup that is poured out for you
is the promise of God, made in my blood.
Whenever you drink it, remember me."

Loving God, we rejoice in the gift of your grace,
remembering Christ's life and death,
proclaiming his resurrection,
waiting in hope for his coming again.
Grant that, in praise and thanksgiving,
we may so offer ourselves to you
that our lives may proclaim the mystery of faith:

Christ has died.
Christ is risen.
Christ will come again.

Send, O God, your Holy Spirit upon us and upon these gifts,
that all who share in this loaf and cup
may be the body of Christ:
light, life, and love in this world.
In this hope and as your people, we praise you.

Through Christ, with Christ, and in Christ,
in the unity of the Holy Spirit,
all glory is yours, God most holy,
now and forever. ***Amen.***[219]

EUCHARISTIC PRAYER 2

Holy God, Holy One, Holy Three!
Before all that is, you were God.
    Outside all we know, you are God.
        After all is finished, you will be God.
Archangels sound the trumpets,
    Angels teach us their song,
        Saints pull us into your presence.

And this is our song:
Holy, holy, holy . . .

Holy God, Holy One, Holy Three!
You beyond the galaxies,
    You under the oceans,
        You inside the leaves,
You pouring down rain,
    You opening the flowers,
        You feeding the insects,
You giving us your image,
    You carrying us through the waters,
        You holding us in the night;
Your smile on Sarah and Abraham,
    Your hand with Moses and Miriam,
        Your words through Deborah and Isaiah,
You lived as Jesus among us,
    Healing, teaching, dying, rising,
        Inviting us to your feast.

In the night in which he was betrayed he took bread, and gave thanks, broke it, and gave it to his disciples, saying:

"Take and eat; this is my body, given for you.
Do this for the remembrance of me."

Again, after supper, he took the cup, gave thanks,
and gave it for all to drink, saying:
"This cup is the new covenant in my blood,
shed for you and for all people for the forgiveness of sin.
Do this for the remembrance of me."

Holy God, we remember your Son,

His life with the humble,
His death among the wretched,
His resurrection for us all:
Your wisdom our guide,
Your justice our strength,
Your grace our path to rebirth.

And so we cry, Mercy:
Mercy!

And so we cry, Glory:
Glory!

And so we cry, Blessing:
Blessing!

Holy God, we beg for your Spirit:
Enliven this bread,
Awaken this body,
Pour us out for each other.
Transfigure our minds,
Ignite your church,
Nourish the life of the earth.
Make us, while many, united,
Make us, though broken, whole,
Make us, despite death, alive.

And so we cry, Come, Holy Spirit:
Come, Holy Spirit!

And so the church shouts, Come, Holy Spirit:
Come, Holy Spirit!

And so the earth pleads, Come, Holy Spirit:
Come, Holy Spirit!

You, Holy God, Holy One, Holy Three,
Our Life, our Mercy, our Might,
    Our Table, our Food, our Server,
        Our Rainbow, our Ark, our Dove,
Our Sovereign, our Water, our Wine,
    Our Light, our Treasure, our Tree,
        Our Way, our Truth, our Life.
You, Holy God, Holy One, Holy Three!

Praise now,
    Praise tomorrow,
        Praise forever.

And so we cry, Amen, amen:
Amen, amen![220]

EUCHARISTIC PRAYER 3

The Lord be with you.

And also with you.

Lift up your hearts.

We lift them to the Lord.

Let us give thanks to the Lord our God.

It is right to give our thanks and praise.

We praise you and we bless you, holy and gracious God,
source of life abundant.
From before time you made ready the creation.
Your Spirit moved over the deep
and brought all things into being:
sun, moon, and stars;
earth, winds, and waters;
and every living thing.
You made us in your image,
and taught us to walk in your ways.
But we rebelled against you, and wandered far away;
and yet, as a mother cares for her children,
you would not forget us.
Time and again you called us
to live in the fullness of your love.

And so this day we join with saints and angels
in the chorus of praise that rings through eternity,
lifting our voices to magnify you as we sing (say):

Holy, holy, holy Lord, God of power and might,
heaven and earth are full of your glory.
Hosanna in the highest.
Blessed is the one who comes in the name of the Lord.
Hosanna in the highest.

Glory and honor and praise to you, holy and living God.
To deliver us from the power of sin and death
and to reveal the riches of your grace,
you looked with favor upon Mary, your willing servant,
that she might conceive and bear a son,
Jesus, the holy child of God.
Living among us, Jesus loved us.
He broke bread with outcasts and sinners,
healed the sick, and proclaimed good news to the poor.
He yearned to draw all the world to himself,
yet we were heedless to his call to walk in love.
Then the time came for him to complete upon the cross
the sacrifice of his life,
and to be glorified in you.

On the night before he died for us,
Jesus was at table with his friends.
He took bread, gave thanks to you,
broke it, and gave it to them, and said:
"Take, eat:
This is my body, which is given for you.
Do this for the remembrance of me."
As supper was ending, Jesus took the cup of wine.
Again, he gave thanks to you,
gave it to them, and said:
"Drink this, all of you:
This is my blood of the new covenant,
which is poured out for you and for all
for the forgiveness of sins.
Whenever you drink it,
do this in remembrance of me."

Now gathered at your table, O God of all creation,
and remembering Christ, crucified and risen,

who was and is and is to come,
we offer to you our gifts of bread and wine,
and ourselves, a living sacrifice.

Pour out your Spirit upon these gifts
that they may be the body and blood of Christ.
Breathe your Spirit over the whole earth
and make us your new creation,
the body of Christ given for the world you have made.

In the fullness of time bring us, with (__________ and) all your saints,
from every tribe and language and people and nation,
to feast at the banquet prepared
from the foundation of the world.

Through Christ and with Christ and in Christ,
in unity with the Holy Spirit,
to you be honor, glory, and praise, for ever and ever. ***Amen.***[221]

ACKNOWLEDGMENTS

As we come to the end of this book of liturgies addressing the many faces of lament, it is with great gratitude that we acknowledge the locations, colleagues, friends, churches, funding sources, libraries, websites, and other resources that have contributed to this book. Truly it has been a community undertaking with tremendous participation as our list of thank-yous will confirm.

The book had as its genesis a question, a place, and a virus. Following the publication of *God's Good Earth: Praise and Prayer for Creation*, we asked the question at the conclusion of a workshop on the book: "What topic is missing from this collection of fifty-two liturgies that you would like to see?" Talitha Arnold, a participant, answered, "Lament." We carried that response in our hearts waiting for a time and place to address it.

The place was the Collegeville Institute at St. John's Abbey and University in Minnesota where we were residential scholars for the spring semester of 2020, during the first six months of the COVID pandemic. We were so profoundly affected by the rolling out of COVID with all its questions, uncertainties, and restrictions, that we abandoned the projects we had intended to pursue as we struggled to understand what was happening to our nation, our world, and ourselves. So, our thanks go to the Collegeville Institute for providing the perfect location for reflection and writing, and to Talitha for inadvertently giving us the subject—lament.

It is harder to show gratitude for COVID, which produced so much death, dislocation, and destruction, but this much we can say: COVID brought us face to face with our own mortality and the precariousness and fragility of life, while it also showed us what resilience, hope, and even joy look like.

We thank the authors of hymns, litanies, prayers, and reflections whose works constitute the contents of the book. We are especially grateful for friends and colleagues who contributed their original works without charge, in particular the following: Talitha Arnold; Alla Renée Bozarth; Catherine de Vinck; Marie Hause; René McGraw, OSB; and Pat White Horse-Carda.

The following churches, organizations, groups, and individuals also contributed works *gratis:* Olga Aivazovska; *America: The Jesuit Review*; Anglican Fellowship of Prayer; Arthur Rank Centre; Ateliers et Presses de Taizé; Peter Bierer; Melissa Bills; Bishops United Against Gun Violence; Norman E. Brookes; Broughton Publishing; Robyn Brown-Hewitt; Frederic and Mary Ann Brussat; The Bulletin of the Atomic Scientists; Helene Burns; CAFOD; Caritas, Aotearoa, New Zealand; Caritas, Philippines; Catholic Charities USA; Chalice Press; Christian Aid; The Church of the Province of New Zealand; Creation Justice Ministries; Angelika Dawson; Antonio De Loera-Brust; Anne Edison-Albright; ELCA; The Episcopal Diocese of Maine; Dorothy Fontaine; Fortress Press; Sister Ruth Fox, OSB; Future Church; David Gambrell; Carolyn Winfrey Gillette; Gripping Films Productions; John G. Hamilton; Simon Hansford; Bill Harder; Lisa Sharon Harper; Peter Healy; Jamie Holmes; Chris Huber; Wilma T. Jakobsen; Patty Jenkins; Elizabeth Kaeton; Sari Kaufman; Valerie Kingsbury; Heather Klinger; Laurie Kraus; Stephen T. Lane; Columba Macbeth-Green; Terry MacKenzie, SHCJ; Father James Martin, SJ; Don McKim; Mennonite Central Committee, BC; Ben Namakin; Tweedy Sombrero Navarrete; The Office of His Holiness the Dalai Lama; Orbis Books; Gunther Peck; Carol Penner; The Presbyterian Outlook Foundation; Robert A. Raines; Gail Ramshaw; Yale Divinity School *Reflections*; Anna E. Rossi; *Sojourners*; Rebecca Solnit; Spill the Beans Resources Team; SpiritualityandPractice.com; William Stokes; Mahogany S. Thomas; Greta Thunberg; Michelle L. Torigian; United States Conference of Catholic Bishops; Uniting Church in Australia; Thomas L. Weitzel; Westminster John Knox Press; Calhoun Wick; Woniya Wakan (Holy Spirit) Episcopal Church; World Vision; Almeda M. Wright; and *YES! Magazine*.

Every effort has been made to identify all the texts used in this book and to secure permission to publish and/or reprint. If we have nonetheless erred in the acknowledgments or infringed on any copyrighted materials, we offer our apologies.

We are indebted to Walter Brueggemann, the renowned biblical scholar, who contributed the insightful foreword. Walter's work over a lifetime has enhanced our understanding of the concept of lament, especially in the psalms, and we are honored that he is part of this book.

We are indebted to the Partner Parishes across the country that used the liturgies in a variety of settings, giving us their feedback and making this a truly a communal project: First Congregational Church, Columbus, Ohio; Holy Trinity Church, Middletown, CT; St. Thomas Church, Alton, RI; Cheyenne River Episcopal Mission, Eagle Butte, SD; Christ Church, Muncie, Indiana; Zion Church, North Branford, CT; St. Barnabas Church, Falmouth, MA; Christ Church, Aspen, CO; St. Paul's Church, Brookings, SD; St. Ann's Church, Old Lyme, CT; St. Peter's Church, Cheshire, CT; and St. Mark's Church, Mystic, CT. We thank their rectors, pastors, and congregations, particularly: Tim Ahrens, Mary Barnett, Bettine Bessier, Ellen and Kurt Huber, Paul Jacobson, Lucy LaRocca, Bill Lupfer, Will Mebane, Larry Ort, Chuck Berry, Anita Schell, Sandy Stayner, and Adam Thomas.

Helene Burns, John Hennigar-Shuh, and Ellen and Kurt Huber contributed both content and critique to the liturgy "Education for Extinction."

Special gratitude is reserved for our own congregation, St. Ann's Church in Old Lyme, Connecticut. When we were locked in our homes over the COVID period, the Creation Care Group held weekly services outdoors in the church's memorial garden. However harsh the weather, even in the freezing days of January and February, we regularly met on a Wednesday afternoon, using services from *God's Good Earth*. For over a year these were the church's only in-person services. The group tested the new liturgies for *God's Good Earth in Crisis*, and St. Ann's Church became the book's main sponsor. We particularly thank the regular participants of the Creation Care Group: Beth Bickley, Sue Joffray, Margo Valentine, Charlie Potts, Lindy Lyman, Steve MacAusland, Pat Hames, Bill Weisert, Alden Rockwell Murphy, Liz Jacobwitz, Carole Lamourine, Jan Cornelius, Jean Read, Liz Zeman, Mac Mummert, Judy Lovlace, Jill Whitney, June Davison, and Anita Schell, the rector, who organized and led the services.

The Diocese of Connecticut awarded us a grant from Companions in Mission for Publishing and Communication, with special thanks to William Schrull, the committee chair. The Episcopal Church's Taskforce on Creation Care and Environmental Racism honored us with a grant. Special thanks to Stephanie Johnson, taskforce chair; Melanie Mullen, the director of Reconciliation Justice and Creation Care; and Phoebe Chatfield, program associate for Creation Care and Justice in the Presiding Bishop's Office. We feel very supported by the Episcopal Church, our home church, our diocese, and by the church nationally.

We have this book to share due to our amazing publishers, Wipf and Stock. In particular we thank James Stock, the CEO, who paved the way for us; Matthew Wimer, the managing editor, who led us through a myriad of details; and the Reverend Robin Parry, our editor.

We have tremendous gratitude for Marie Hause who has tirelessly searched for original copyright holders and managed the permissions process, and much more. When we inadvertently repeated a prayer or litany from *God's Good Earth* or within this volume, Marie spotted it. This is certainly a better book because of Marie's efforts.

Further invaluable assistance was given—especially in the latter stages of the proofing—by the Reverend Cynthia Thun Willauer and the Reverend Patricia M. Hames.

The champions of Mother Earth are legion and we are grateful to them all. We are dedicating this book to those closest to us whose lives and works we know well and who have touched us personally and deeply. Mary Evelyn Tucker and John Grim are generally recognized as the founders of the field of religion and ecology, which began with a series of conferences at Harvard in the 1990s and then moved to Yale. As a result of their pioneering work, there are now sixteen graduate programs in religion and ecology throughout the country. Margaret Bullitt-Jonas is an Episcopal priest and Missioner for Creation Care in the Episcopal Diocese of Western Massachusetts and the Southern New England Conference of the United Church of Christ. She is a writer and tireless climate activist who takes her passion for climate justice to the streets and public square. She speaks at climate justice rallies, public hearings and vigils, and climate marches. Talitha Arnold and Anita Louise Schell are inspired and inspiring parish clergy whose passion for a just society and healthy planet is reflected in public worship in their churches and in their wider communities. Talitha is the senior minister of the United Church of Santa Fe, which, guided by her leadership, has tripled church membership. She is also a writer and a nationally recognized leader in the United Church of Christ. Anita Louise Schell, the rector of St. Ann's Church in Old Lyme, Connecticut, came to the parish just before COVID unleashed its chaos on the nation with all its attendant isolation and hardships. Nonetheless, Anita navigated online and outdoor worship throughout it all. She is also the chair of the Creation Care Ministry Network of the Episcopal Diocese of Connecticut.

Poets nurture our lives and show us a glimpse of eternity. The final dedication of this book is to Alla Renée Bozarth and to the memory of Catherine de Vinck, friends for many years who have both contributed reflections to this book. Their poetry is life-giving; it speaks to our deepest longings; it expresses the almost inexpressible, where in the words of Alla:

> . . . the soul touches softly or rolls suddenly
> into a lost-at-sea funnel to bottomless, endless
> eternity, beyond water and rock and fire,
> beyond sun and moon and into
> something like light and something like
> a nourishing chalice of endless love,
> and something like the sheerest, deepest,
> way of being alive.[222]

SUPPLEMENTARY HYMNS

Hymn / Author	Meter	Tune
All creatures of our God most high		
St. Francis of Assisi	8.8.4.4.8.8 and refrain	LASST UNS ERFREUEN
All praise to you, O God of all creation		
Omer Westendorf	11.10.11.10.11.10	FINLANDIA
As conflicts rage and lives are lost		
Jeffery Rowthorn	LM	BRESLAU
As waters rise around us		
Mary Louise Bringle	8.7.8.7 and refrain	BRYN CALFARIA
Beauty for brokenness		
Graham Kendrick	6.4.6.4 D and refrain	GOD OF THE POOR
Blest are the innocents		
Sylvia Dunstan	10.10.10.10	BETHLEHEM'S OWN
Children from your vast creation		
David A. Robb	8.7.8.7 D	BLAENWERN
Children of God, reach out to one another!		
John Greenleaf Whittier	11.10.11.10	DONNE SECOURS
Christ has changed the world's direction!		
Shirley Erena Murray	8.7.8.7.6.7	MICHAEL
Christ, you call us all to service		
Joy F. Patterson	8.7.8.7 D	IN BABILONE
Community of Christ		
Shirley Erena Murray	6.6.8.4 D	LEONI
Creating God, your fingers trace		
Jeffery Rowthorn	LM	DEUS TUORUM MILITUM

Creative God, you spread the earth		
Ruth Duck	CMD	KINGSFOLD
Dream on, dream on		
Hae Jong Kim	Irregular Meter	DREAM ON
Everything that has voice, sing for peace		
Shirley Erena Murray	6.3.3.6.3.3.7.7.6.3	SING FOR PEACE
For everyone born a place at the table		
Shirley Erena Murray	11.10.11.10 and refrain	TABLESONG
For the fruit of all creation		
Fred Pratt Green	8.4.8.4.8.8.8.4	AR HYD Y NOS
For the healing of the nations		
Fred Kaan	8.7.8.7.8.7	REGENT SQUARE
God is still speaking		
Barbara Hamm	11.12.12.12	BRANDON
Go, be justice to God's people		
Martin Willett	8.7.8.7 D	NETTLETON
God in his love for us lent us this planet		
Fred Pratt Green	10.10.11.10	ECOLOGY
God, whose farm is all creation		
John Arlott	8.7.8.7	STUTTGART
God, you see your loved creation		
Herman Stuempfle Jr.	8.7.8.7	RESTORATION
Hear the land crying		
Norman Habel	5.5.5.4 D	BUNESSAN
Hope of the World		
Georgia Harkness	11.10.11.10	DONNE SECOURS
How long, O God, how long		
Thomas H. Troeger	SM	LITTLE MARLBOROUGH
I am standing waiting		
Shirley Erena Murray	6.5.5 D	KING'S WESTON
I, the Lord of sea and sky		
Daniel Schutte	7.7.7.4 D and refrain	HERE I AM
In an age of twisted values		
Martin Leckebusch	8.7.8.7 D	EBENEZER

In the beginning, God played		
Andrew Pratt	11.10.11.10	WAS LEBET
In the midst of new dimensions		
Julian B. Rush	8.7.8.7 and refrain	NEW DIMENSIONS
It is God who holds the nations in the hollow of his hand		
Fred Pratt Green	15.15.15.7	VISION
Jesu, Jesu, fill us with your love		
Tom Colvin	7. 7. 9 and refrain	CHEREPONI
Jesus entered Egypt		
Adam M. L. Tice	6.5.6.5 D	KING'S WESTON
Join the song of praise and protest		
Michael Forster	8.7.8.7 D	BLAENWERN
Let there be peace on earth		
Sy Miller and Jill Jackson	Irregular Meter	WORLD PEACE
Light dawns on a weary world		
Mary Louise Bringle	7.6.6.7.8 and refrain	TEMPLE OF PEACE
Make me a channel of your peace		
Attributed to St. Francis, adapted by Sebastian Temple	Irregular Meter	MAKE ME A CHANNEL OF YOUR PEACE
Maker God who breathed creation		
Jacque B. Jones	8.7.8.7 and refrain	TRUST ALONE
Night and day this planet sings		
Thomas H. Troeger	7.7.7.7 D	SALZBURG
O day of peace that dimly shines		
Carl P. Daw Jr.	LMD	JERUSALEM
O God of all creation		
Michael Forster	13.13.13.13.13.13.	THAXTED
O God of every nation		
William W. Reid Jr.	7.6.7.6 D	LLANGLOFFAN
O God of love, O God of peace		
Henry W. Baker	LM	ERHALT UNS, HERR
O God, your justice towers		
Herman Stuempfle Jr.	7.6.7.6 D	NYLAND
O for a world where everyone		
Miriam Therese Winter	CM	AZMON

O who will speak for justice		
Betsy Phillips Fisher	7.6.7.6 D	LLANGLOFFAN
Praise God for the harvest		
Brian Wren	11.11.11.11	STOWEY
Restless weaver, ever spinning		
O. I. Cricket Harrison	8.7.8.7 D	BEACH SPRING
Shall we gather at the river		
Robert Lowry	8.7.8.7 and refrain	KINGSFOLD
Sing a new world into being		
Mary Louise Bringle	8.7.8.7 D	HYMN TO JOY
Sing praise to God on mountain tops		
John L. Bell and Graham Maule	8.7.8.7 D	THE VICAR OF BRAY
Teach us, O loving heart of Christ		
Shirley Erena Murray	CM	DAVIDSON
The garden needs our tending now		
Mary Louise Bringle	8.6.8.6.8.8 and refrain	UNE JEUNE PUCELLE
The kingdom of God is justice and joy		
Bryn A. Rees	10.10.11.11	LAUDATE DOMINUM
The whole creation is a song		
Jeffery Rowthorn	8.8.8.8 LM	O WALY WALY
There is a balm in Gilead		
	Irregular Meter and refrain	BALM IN GILEAD
There is no child so small		
Shirley Erena Murray	6.7.7.6	LEAST CHILD
This is my song		
Lloyd Stone	11.10.11.10.11.10	FINLANDIA
Till all the jails are empty		
Carl P. Daw Jr.	7.6.7.6 D and refrain	WORK TO DO
Touch that soothes and heals		
Mary Louise Bringle	8.7.8.7 D and refrain	GENEVA
You formed Creation by your Word		
Jacque B. Jones	8.6.8.6 D	NOEL
Walls mark our boundaries and keep us apart		
Ruth Duck	10.10.10.10 and refrain	PENROSE

We cannot own the sunlit sky		
Ruth Duck	8.7.8.7 D	HOW CAN I KEEP FROM SINGING
We shall overcome		
African American Spiritual	Irregular Meter	WE SHALL OVERCOME
When children wake to tears		
Mary Louise Bringle	11.11.11.5	ISTE CONFESSOR
When in awe of God's creation		
Jane Parker Huber	8.7.8.7 D	HYFRYDOL
When the present holds no promise		
Thomas H. Troeger	8.7.8.7 D	BEACH SPRING
When the sword and spear are broken		
Adam M.L.Tice	8.7.8.7.8.7.7	CWM RHONDDA
When we look and see		
Pete Seeger and Lorre Wyatt	Irregular Meter	GOD'S COUNTING ON ME
Where armies scourge the countryside		
Herman Stuempfle Jr.	8.6.8.6.8.6	MORNING GLORY
Where cross the crowded ways of life		
Frank Mason North and Ruth Duck	LM	GERMANY
Will the circle be unbroken		
Tony E. Alonso	8.7.8.7 D	TONY E. ALONSO *Composer*
Wind of the Spirit		
Herman Stuempfle Jr.	11.10.11.10.11.10	FINLANDIA

ABOUT THE EDITORS

Anne W. Rowthorn (1939–2023) was a writer specializing in ecology and eco-spirituality. During her travels and research, she collected literature from great cultures and religions of the world, compiling them into her books, including *God's Good Earth* (co-written with Jeffery Rowthorn) and *Earth and All the Stars*. She also authored *The Wisdom of John Muir* (Wilderness Press). Her book *Your Daily Life Is Your Temple* was designated a best spirituality book by Spirituality & Practice (spiritualityandpractice.com).

Jeffery W. Rowthorn, born in Newport, Wales, is a retired Episcopal bishop and hymnographer. His early career was spent in parish ministry in England. Moving to the United States, he then worked at two seminaries: Union Theological Seminary and Berkeley Divinity School. Elected bishop in the Episcopal Church, he served in the Diocese of Connecticut and as bishop of the Convocation in Europe. His hymns have been widely published and he has compiled three hymnals.

ENDNOTES

INTRODUCTION

1 “Nobody Knows the Trouble I’ve Seen.” Public domain.

2 Walter Brueggemann, *The Message of the Psalms* (Minneapolis: Augsburg, 1984), 67.

3 Donna M. Cox, “The Power of a Song in a Strange Land,” *The Conversation*, February 13, 2020, accessed April 20, 2021, https://theconversation.com/the-power-of-a-song-in-a-strange-land-129969.

4 Frederick Douglass, *Narrative of the Life of Frederick Douglass, an American Slave* (Boston: Anti-Slavery Office, 1845), 14–15. Internet Archive, https://archive.org/details/narrativeoflife1845doug.

5 Walter Brueggemann, “The Costly Loss of Lament,” in *The Psalms: The Life of Faith*, edited by Patrick D. Miller (Minneapolis: Fortress, 1995), 102 and 108.

6 Walter Brueggemann, *The Message of the Psalms* (Minneapolis: Augsburg, 1984), 67.

7 Soong-Chan Rah, *Prophetic Lament: A Call for Justice in Troubled Times* (Downers Grove, IL: InterVarsity, 2015), 29.

8 Emilie M. Townes, “Lament and Hope: Defying the Hot Mess,” *Reflections*, Fall 2019, https://reflections.yale.edu/article/resistance-and-blessing-women-ministry-and-yds/lament-and-hope-defying-hot-mess.

9 Margret Bullitt-Jonas, in “Preaching Climate Justice: A Conversation with Jim Antal and Margaret Bullitt-Jonas,” *Reviving Creation*, September 16, 2022, accessed September 26, 2022, https://revivingcreation.org/preaching-climate-justice-a-conversation-with-jim-antal-and-margaret-bullitt-jonas/.

1. EXTREME HEAT

10 Rebecca Solnit, "Jurassic Ballot: When Corporations Ruled the Earth," *TomDispatch*, October 24, 2010, https://tomdispatch.com/rebecca-solnit-invasion-of-the-democracy-crushers/. © 2010 Rebecca Solnit. Used by permission.

11 Anne Knighton, "Eternal God, you are the power . . . ," in *Oceans of Prayer*, compiled by Maureen Edwards and Jan S. Pickard (Nutfield, UK: National Christian Education Council, UK, 1991), 11. © 1991 National Christian Education Council, UK. RE Today Services. www.retoday.org.uk. www.ibraglobal.org. Used by permission.

12 "God of all creation, we cry out to you . . . ," in "Service of Prayer and Conversation in the Midst of Drought," arranged by Bill Harder, Evangelical Lutheran Church in Canada Synod of Alberta and the Territories, accessed February 26, 2021, https://www.albertasynod.ca/wp-content/uploads/2012/02/Service-of-Prayer-and-Conversation-in-the-Midst-of-Drought.pdf, alt. Used by permission of Bill Harder.

13 Isaiah 35:1–10 from Confraternity of Christian Doctrine, *The New American Bible*, rev. ed. (Wichita, KS: Catholic Bible Publishers, 2011).

14 Anne Rowthorn, "Someone's Suffering from Extreme Heat," © 2021 Anne Rowthorn.

15 From Kathy Baughman McLeod, "Heat Waves," in "The Election Outcome Will Make Sweeping Climate Action Harder," by Bill McKibben, *The New Yorker*, November 4, 2020. Bill McKibben, The New Yorker © Condé Nast. Used by permission.

16 Anne Rowthorn, "Holy God of Earth, Wind, Heat and Fire," © 2021 Anne Rowthorn.

17 "God of opportunity and change . . . ," in Church of the Province of New Zealand, *A New Zealand Prayer Book—He Karakia Mihinare o Aotearoa* (Auckland, New Zealand: William Collins, 1989), 135. © 1989 The Provincial Secretary, The Church of the Province of New Zealand, Box 2148, Rotorua. Used by permission.

18 Norman Habel, "Wise Up, Wise Up, You Christians," in *Habel Hymns, Vol. 3: Songs in Support of the Eco-Reformation in 2017 and On-Going Earthcare*, 2016, http://www.earth-link.org.au/userfiles/Habel-Hymns-3.pdf. © 2008 Norman Habel.

19 Alan Gaunt, "Take Courage," in *Praise God* (London: Baptist Union, 1980), 166, from Alan Gaunt, *New Prayers for Worship* (John Paul Press, 1972).

2. DROUGHT

20 "God of earth and sky . . . ," in "Service of Prayer and Conversation in the Midst of Drought," arranged by Bill Harder, Evangelical Lutheran Church in Canada Synod of Alberta and the Territories, accessed February 26, 2021, https://www.albertasynod.ca/wp-content/uploads/2012/02/Service-of-Prayer-and-Conversation-in-the-Midst-of-Drought.pdf, alt. Used by permission of Bill Harder.

21 "O God, we pray for those places . . . ," from *With All God's People: The New Ecumenical Prayer Cycle*, compiled by John Carden (Geneva: World Council of Churches, 1989), 342, alt. Original source unknown.

22 Columba Macbeth-Green, "Prayer for Rain," in "Prayers for the Drought," National Council of Churches in Australia, August 28, 2018, https://www.ncca.org.au/prayer/prayer-for-our-troubled-world/item/1453-prayers-for-the-drought, alt. Used by permission of Columba Macbeth-Green.

23 Jeremiah 14:1–6, 9b from Confraternity of Christian Doctrine, *The New American Bible*, rev. ed. (Wichita, KS: Catholic Bible Publishers, 2011).

24 Simon Hansford, "We pray for the land . . . ," in "Prayers for the Drought," *National Council of Churches in Australia*, August 28, 2018, https://www.ncca.org.au/prayer/prayer-for-our-troubled-world/item/1453-prayers-for-the-drought, alt. Used by permission of Simon Hansford.

25 From Caroline Henderson, June 30, 1935 letter, in Caroline Henderson, *Letters from the Dust Bowl*, edited by Alvin O. Turner (Norman, OK: University of Oklahoma Press, 2001), 147–50. © University of Oklahoma Press. Used by permission.

26 Arthur Rank Centre, "The Farming Community," in *Harvest for the World: A Christian Aid/CAFOD Worship Anthology on Sharing in the Work of Creation*, edited by and compiled by Geoffrey Duncan, 2nd ed. (Norwich, UK: Canterbury, 2004), 55, alt. © The Arthur Rank Centre. Used by permission.

27 "Creating God, today we pray . . . ," in *Celebrate God's Presence: A Book of Services for The United Church of Canada* (Etobicoke, ON: United Church Publishing House, 2000), 615–16, no. 21T008, alt. Author unknown.

28 Isaac Watts, "O God, Our Help in Ages Past." Public domain.

3. WILDFIRE

29 Psalm 80:14–16a from *The Inclusive Bible: The First Egalitarian Translation* (Lanham, MD: Rowman and Littlefield, 2007). © Future Church. Used by permission.

30 Carol Penner, "Wildfire Prayer," *Leading in Worship*, December 2, 2018, https://leadinginworship.com/2018/12/wildfire-prayer/. © Carol Penner, leadinginworship.com. All rights reserved. Used by permission.

31 Glenn Davies, "A Prayer for Australia in Drought and Fire," in Russell Powell, "Prayer for Protection amid Bushfire Emergency," *Sydney Anglicans*, Anglican Diocese of Sydney, January 2, 2020, accessed May 16, 2023, https://sydneyanglicans.net/news/prayer-for-protection-amid-bushfire-emergency, alt.

32 Talitha Arnold, "Prayer for All Creatures in a Time of Drought and Fire," in Sing for Earth, Pray for Earth, Act for Earth (conference program), United Church of Santa Fe, March 21–23, 2014. Used by permission.

33 From Jamie Holmes, "The Paradise Diaspora: An Alum's First-hand Account," *Yale Divinity School*, January 8, 2020, accessed June 8, 2023, https://divinity.yale.edu/news/paradise-diaspora-alum-s-first-hand-account. With revisions by Jamie Holmes. © 2020 Jamie Holmes. Used by permission of Jamie Holmes and Yale Divinity School.

34 From Antonio De Loera-Brust, "A Prayer for Wildfire Victims," *America: The Jesuit Review*, October 20, 2017, https://www.americamagazine.org/faith/2017/10/20/prayer-california-fire-victims-oregon-washington, alt. Used by permission of Antonio De Loera-Brust and *America: The Jesuit Review*.

35 From Antonio De Loera-Brust, "A Prayer for Wildfire Victims," *America: The Jesuit Review*, October 20, 2017, https://www.americamagazine.org/faith/2017/10/20/prayer-california-fire-victims-oregon-washington, alt. Used by permission of Antonio De Loera-Brust and *America: The Jesuit Review*.

36 Peter Bierer, "A Prayer during the Australian Bushfires," *America: The Jesuit Review*, January 7, 2020, accessed October 5, 2020, https://www.americamagazine.org/faith/2020/01/07/prayer-during-australian-bushfires, alt. Used by permission of Peter Bierer and *America: The Jesuit Review*.

37 Carolyn Winfrey Gillette, "A God of Mighty Wind and Flame," © 2007 Carolyn Winfrey Gillette. All rights reserved. www.carolynshymns.com. carolynshymns@gmail.com. Used by permission.

38 "May the presence of God . . . ," in *Chalice Worship*, edited by Colbert S. Cartwright and O. I. Cricket Harrison (St. Louis: Chalice, 1997), 444, no. 785, alt. From *1987 United Methodist Clergywomen's Consultation Resource Book*, 67. Please use this credit line in lieu of seeking written permission.

4. WILD WINDS

39 From Pope Francis, *Laudato si*, accessed December 1, 2022, Vatican.va, 233. © Dicastero per la Comunicazione-Libreria Editrice Vaticana. Used by permission.

40 "God of power . . . ," in Church of the Province of New Zealand, *A New Zealand Prayer Book—He Karakia Mihinare o Aotearoa* (Auckland, New Zealand: William Collins, 1989), 541. © 1989 The Provincial Secretary, The Church of the Province of New Zealand, Box 2148, Rotorua. Used by permission.

41 "Prayer for Philippines Storm Victims," St. Mary's Parish, website of St. Mary's Parish, Winnipeg, Manitoba, accessed February 1, 2021, http://stmarypncc.ca/?page_id=4896, alt.

42 Psalm 121 from *The Inclusive Bible: The First Egalitarian Translation* (Lanham, MD: Rowman and Littlefield, 2007). © Future Church. Used by permission.

43 Thomas L. Weitzel, "Exhortation and Litany at the Beginning of the Hurricane & Tornado Seasons," in Thomas L. Weitzel, *Prayer Book for the Hurricane and Tornado Seasons*, on Liturgy by TLW, accessed February 22, 2021, http://www.liturgybytlw.com/OccChs/Hurrican.html#Beginning%20of%20Season, alt. © T. L. Weitzel (LiturgyByTLW.com). Used by permission.

44 Antonio Labiao, "Caritas Philippines Would Welcome a Global Vision for the Future as Climate Emergencies Increase," Caritas, December 12, 2020, accessed January 25, 2021, https://www.caritas.org/2020/12/global-vision-for-climate/. Used by permission of Caritas Philippines.

45 James Martin, SJ, "A Hurricane Prayer," *America: The Jesuit Review*, October 28, 2012, accessed January 23, 2023, https://www.americamagazine.org/faith/2012/10/28/hurricane-prayer. Used by permission of Father James Martin, SJ, and *America: The Jesuit Review*.

46 Heather Klinger, "Merciful Counselor, we grieve . . ." in Heather Klinger, "Matthew 25: Prayer for Refugees, Disaster Survivors," World Vision, last updated May 12, 2021, https://www.worldvision.org/refugees-news-stories/pray-refugees-disaster-survivors. Used by permission of Heather Klinger and World Vision.

47 Adam M. L. Tice, "In Floods of Chaos," © 2009 GIA Publications, Inc. All rights reserved. Used by permission.

5. FLOOD

48 Nahum 1:7 from *The Inclusive Bible: The First Egalitarian Translation* (Lanham, MD: Rowman and Littlefield, 2007). © Future Church. Used by permission.

49 Edward Hays, "Tuesday Evening Prayer," in Edward Hays, *Prayers for a Planetary Pilgrim* (Easton, KS: Forest of Peace, 1988), 65, alt. Excerpted from *Prayers for a Planetary Pilgrim* by Edward M. Hays, © 1989, 2008. Used with the permission of the publisher, Forest of Peace, an imprint of Ave Maria Press®, Inc., Notre Dame, Indiana 46556. www.forestofpeace.com.

50 Christian Aid, UK, "Faithful and loving God . . . ," Christian Aid, accessed March 25, 2021, https://www.christianaid.org.uk/resources/prayers-south-asia-floods, alt. Used by permission of Christian Aid.

51 Psalm 29:3–11 from *The Ecumenical Grail Psalter* (Chicago: GIA, 2015). Used by permission of the United States Conference of Catholic Bishops.

52 John G. Hamilton, "A Prayer When Waters Are Rising," PCUSA, accessed March 28, 2023, https://pda.pcusa.org/site_media/media/uploads/pda/pdfs/flooding.pdf, alt. Used by permission of John G. Hamilton.

53 From "Flood City," by Jennifer Oladipo, which appeared in the July/Aug 2015 issue of *Orion Magazine*, alt. Used by permission of *Orion Magazine*.

54 Laurie Kraus, "Prayer Following Gulf Coast Flooding," Presbyterian Disaster Assistance, accessed October 21, 2020, https://pda.pcusa.org/pda/resource/prayer-following-baton-rouge-gulf-flood/. Used by permission of Laurie Kraus.

55 "Great and merciful God . . . ," from the Alternate Eucharistic Liturgy of the Church of South India. Used by permission of the Church of South India Synod.

56 Carolyn Winfrey Gillette, "When Waters Roar and Foam," © 2012 Carolyn Winfrey Gillette. All rights reserved. www.carolynshymns.com. carolynshymns@gmail.com. Used by permission.

57 "May the strength of God . . . ," attributed to St. Patrick.

6. EARTHQUAKE

58 Psalm 55:22 from *The Inclusive Bible: The First Egalitarian Translation* (Lanham, MD: Rowman and Littlefield, 2007). © Future Church. Used by permission.

59 Wilma T. Jakobsen, "Let Our Cries Come unto You," in "Prayers in Times of Natural Disaster," JesuitResource.org, The Center for Mission and Identity at Xavier University, accessed January 14, 2021, https://www.xavier.edu/jesuitresource/online-resources/prayer-index/prayers-in-times-of-crisis/in-times-of-natural-disaster. Used by permission of Wilma T. Jakobsen.

60 "A Prayer for Victims of the Earthquake," St. Mary's Parish, website of St. Mary's Parish, Winnipeg, Manitoba, accessed February 1, 2021, http://stmarypncc.ca/?page_id=7230.

61 Melissa Bills and Anne Edison-Albright, "God our refuge, we lift . . . ," from Melissa Bills and Anne Edison-Albright, "Worship Resource for the Anniversary of Earthquake in Haiti," Evangelical Lutheran Church in America, ELCA Worship, January 2, 2020, accessed February 23, 2021, https://blogs.elca.org/worship/1374/, alt. Used by permission of Melissa Bills and Anne Edison-Albright.

62 Nicholas Roxburgh, "Nepal Earthquake: Eyewitness Account from Kathmandu," Medium, posted by Christian Aid, April 28, 2015, accessed February 1, 2021, https://medium.com/@ChristianAid/nepal-earthquake-eyewitness-account-from-kathmandu-51baa6da6d6e. Used by permission of Christian Aid.

63 Melissa Bills and Anne Edison-Albright, "God, our refuge and strength . . . ," from Melissa Bills and Anne Edison-Albright, "Worship Resource for the Anniversary of Earthquake in Haiti," Evangelical Lutheran Church in America, ELCA Worship, January 2, 2020, accessed February 23, 2021, https://blogs.elca.org/worship/1374/, alt. Used by permission of Melissa Bills and Anne Edison-Albright.

64 "Holy One, You Are Our Comfort and Strength," Presbyterian Church USA, *Book of Common Worship* (Louisville, KY: Westminster John Knox, 2018), 577. Used by permission of Westminster John Knox Press.

65 Words by Andrew Pratt, "Tectonic Plates beneath the Ocean's Surface," © 2011 Stainer & Bell, Ltd. (Admin. Hope Publishing Company, www.hopepublishing.com). All rights reserved. Used by permission.

66 "Let nothing disturb you . . . ," attributed to St. Teresa of Avila.

7. TSUNAMI

67 From Leonardo Boff, *Way of the Cross—Way of Justice*, translated by John Drury (Maryknoll, NY: Orbis, 1982), 37. © Orbis Books. Used by permission.

68 Anne Rowthorn, "Dear God and Savior of All," © 2021 Anne Rowthorn.

69 William Stokes, "A Prayer for the Victims of Katrina," *The Text This Week*, http://www.textweek.com/response/following_litany_and_prayer.htm, alt. Used by permission of the author.

70 "We tremble as the earth reels and rocks . . . ," based on Psalm 18:3, 7–8, incorporating material from Christian Aid, UK, "O God hold those who are hurting . . . ," Christian Aid, 18 December 2018, accessed February 21, 2021, https://www.christianaid.org.uk/resources/prayer-indonesian-earthquake-and-tsunami. Used by permission of Christian Aid.

71 From Almeda M. Wright, "Creating, Sustaining, and Persisting: An Interview with Almeda Wright," *Reflections* (Fall 2020), https://reflections.yale.edu/article/seeking-light-notes-hope/creating-sustaining-persisting-interview-almeda-wright. Used by permission of the author and Yale Divinity School *Reflections*.

72 Shai Held, "Prayer in the Wake of the Tsunami" (English text), The Open Siddur Project, accessed May 29, 2021, https://opensiddur.org/prayers/collective-welfare/trouble/earthquakes/prayer-in-the-wake-of-the-tsunami/, alt. Shared under Creative Commons Attribution-ShareAlike 4.0 International, https://creativecommons.org/licenses/by-sa/4.0/legalcode. The biblical quotation is from Genesis 9:11.

73 David Gambrell, "Living God, our refuge and strength . . . ," (based on Mark 4), in "Prayers in Times of Trouble and Disaster," PCUSA, accessed October 20, 2020, https://www.pcusa.org/site_media/media/uploads/pda/pdfs/prayersintimesoftroubleanddisaster.pdf. Used by permission of David Gambrell.

74 Norman E. Brookes, "When the Earth's Wild Hidden Forces," © 2010 Norman E. Brookes. Used by permission.

75 Ronald J. Allen and Linda McKiernan-Allen, "Thank you, Lord . . .", in *Chalice Worship*, compiled and edited by Colbert S. Cartwright and O. I. Cricket Harrison (St. Louis, MO: Chalice, 1997), 302, no. 259. By Ronald J. Allen and Linda McKiernan-Allen. © 1997 Chalice Press. Used by permission of Chalice Press.

8. RISING SEAS

76 Michael Perry, Patrick Goodland, and Angela Griffiths, "Thanksgiving for the Universe," in *Prayers for the People, Leader's Edition*, edited by Michael Perry, Patrick Goodland, and Angela Griffiths (London: Marshal Pickering, 1992), 179, no. 10.37. © The Jubilate Group (Admin. Hope Publishing Company, www.hopepublishing.com). All rights reserved. Used by permission.

77 Christina Bechara, "Starting Again," in Caritas, Aotearoa New Zealand, *Climate Change Prayer Booklet* for the Just Water: Climate Change in the Pacific series (Caritas, Aotearoa New Zealand, 2017), accessed March 21, 2023, https://link.caritas.org.nz/Climate-Change-Prayer-Booklet.pdf, alt. Used by permission of Caritas, Aotearoa, New Zealand.

78 Chris Huber, "Lord, may those suffering . . . ," in Chris Huber, "Covering the World in Prayer: Pray for the Asia-Pacific Islands," World Vision, last updated February 26, 2018, https://www.worldvision.org/christian-faith-news-stories/covering-world-prayer-pray-asia-pacific-islands. Used by permission.

79 Anne Rowthorn, "O Holy God of Rolling Seas," © 2021 Anne Rowthorn.

80 Ben Namakin, "The Beauty of my Homeland, Kiribati," posted on the Facebook page "Humans of Kiribati," March 31, 2023, https://www.facebook.com/1571889726417878/posts/kiribati-voices-climate-change-is-not-a-distant-threat-it-is-affecting-real-peop/1912678072339040/. © Ben Namakin. Used by permission.

81 Anne and Jeffery Rowthorn, "God of Islands and Atolls," © 2023 Anne and Jeffery Rowthorn.

82 From Jean-Bertrand Aristide, *In the Parish of the Poor: Writings from Haiti*, translated and edited by Amy Wilentz (Maryknoll, NY: Orbis, 1990), 98–99. © 1993 Orbis Books. Adapted in *Dare to Dream: A Prayer and Worship Anthology from Around the World*, edited by Geoffrey Duncan (London: HarperCollins, 1995), 200, alt. Used by permission.

83 William Whiting, "Eternal Father! Strong to Save." Public domain.

84 Stephen W. Burgess and James D. Righter, "Nothing can separate us . . . ," in *Celebrations for Today* (Nashville: Abingdon, 1977), 61. © 1977 Abingdon Press.

9. BLIZZARD

85 William Shakespeare, *As You Like It*, 2.1.553–56. Open Source Shakespeare, https://www.opensourceshakespeare.org/views/plays/play_view.php?WorkID=asyoulikeit&Act=2&Scene=1&Scope=scene.

86 Psalm 148:7b, 8a from *The Inclusive Bible: The First Egalitarian Translation* (Lanham, MD: Rowman and Littlefield, 2007). © Future Church. Used by permission.

87 "God, our Creator, as we face . . . ," in "Storm Sunday," Australian Version 1, Season of Creation, accessed February 16, 2021, https://seasonofcreation.com/wp-content/uploads/2010/04/liturgy-storm-sunday-1.pdf. © Season of Creation, developed by Norm Habel and the Uniting Church in Australia, Synod of Victoria and Tasmania, 2004, seasonofcreation.com.

88 Anne Rowthorn, "O Holy God of Snow and Rain," © 2021 Anne Rowthorn.

89 Psalm 147:7–9, 16–18 from *The Inclusive Bible: The First Egalitarian Translation* (Lanham, MD: Rowman and Littlefield, 2007). © Future Church. Used by permission.

90 Anne Rowthorn, "As the Driving Snow Gathers," © 2021 Anne Rowthorn.

91 From Ole Edvart Rølvaag, *Giants in the Earth: A Saga of the Prairie*, translated by Lincoln Colcord (New York: Harper & Brothers, 1927), 269–70, 275–76. Public domain.

92 Cal Wick, "In the Midst of Winter," in "Winter Prayers," JesuitResource.org, The Center for Mission and Identity at Xavier University, accessed February 25, 2021, https://www.xavier.edu/jesuitresource/online-resources/prayer-index/winter-prayers. Used by permission of the author.

93 "Traveler's Prayer (*Tefilat HaDerech*)," traditional Jewish prayer.

94 Samuel Longfellow, "Winter Song." Public domain.

95 "Following whatever roads . . . ," author unknown, in Ruth L. Benzel, "Introduction to Zuñi Ceremonialism," in *Forty-Seventh Annual Report of the Bureau of American Ethnology, 1929–1930* (Washington, DC: U.S. Govt. Print Off, 1932), 484. Public domain.

10. PETROLEUM PIPELINES

96 Christian Aid and CAFOD (Catholic Agency for Overseas Development), "A Maasai Prayer," in *Harvest for the World: A Christian Aid/CAFOD Worship Anthology on Sharing in the Work of Creation*, edited and compiled by Geoffrey Duncan, 2nd ed. (Norwich, UK: Canterbury, 2004), 251. © Christian Aid and CAFOD. Used by permission of Christian Aid and CAFOD.

97 "We give you thanks . . . ," in *The Book of Common Prayer* (New York: Church Hymnal Corporation, 1979), 840.

98 Frederic and Mary Ann Brussat, "A Prayer for Protection of Sacred Lands and Waters," Spirituality & Practice: Resources for Spiritual Journeys (SpiritualityandPractice.com), August 24, 2016, https://www.spiritualityandpractice.com/blogs/posts/praying-the-news/421/a-prayer-for-protection-of-sacred-lands-and-waters, alt. Used by permission of SpiritualityandPractice.com.

99 Psalm 136:1–9, 16–17, 21–22 from *The Ecumenical Grail Psalter* (Chicago: GIA, 2015). Used by permission of the United States Conference of Catholic Bishops.

100 Tweedy Sombrero Navarrete, "Let God's Creation Sustain You," in *Environmental Justice with Indigenous People* (Creation Justice Ministries), 9, Creation Justice Ministries, accessed April 13, 2017, http://www.creationjustice.org/uploads/2/5/4/6/25465131/earthday2017_elca.pdf?key=54869765, alt. Used by permission of Tweedy Sombrero Navarrete.

101 From Mark Trahant, "3 Reasons the Standing Rock Sioux Can Stop the Dakota Access Pipeline," *YES!*, August 22, 2016, https://www.yesmagazine.org/democracy/2016/08/22/3-reasons-the-standing-rock-sioux-can-stop-the-dakota-access-pipeline/. This article was originally published by YES! Magazine and is reprinted here with permission.

102 "We remember the dry land . . . ," in "Land Sunday," Australian Version 1, Season of Creation, accessed March 26, 2021, https://seasonofcreation.com/wp-content/uploads/2010/04/liturgy-land-sunday-1.pdf, alt. © Season of Creation, developed by Norm Habel and the Uniting Church in Australia, Synod of Victoria and Tasmania, 2004, seasonofcreation.com.

103 Jim Cotter, "Eternal Spirit . . . ," in The Church of the Province of New Zealand, *A New Zealand Prayer Book – He Karakia Mihinare o Aotearoa* (Auckland: William Collins, 1988), 181, adapted from Jim Cotter, *Prayer at Night* (Sheffield, UK: Cairns, 1988), 42. Used by permission of The Church of the Province of New Zealand. Extract from *Prayer at Night's Approaching* by Jim Cotter is copyright © Jim Cotter 2001, published by Cairns Publications and is reproduced by permission of Hymns Ancient & Modern Ltd, rights@hymnsam.co.uk.

104 Words by Shirley Erena Murray, "Touch the Earth Lightly," © 1992 Hope Publishing Company, www.hopepublishing.com. All rights reserved. Used by permission.

105 Brian Baker, "A Blessing," in Religious AF Camp, *A Black Rock Prayer Book*, 9, http://www.ees1862.org/wp-content/uploads/2019/10/A-Black-Rock-Prayer-Book-2019.pdf. Used by permission of Brian Baker.

11. OCEAN OIL SPILLS

106 "O God, our Creator, as we reflect . . . ," in "Ocean Sunday," Australian Version 1, Season of Creation, accessed March 16, 2021, https://seasonofcreation.com/wp-content/uploads/2010/04/liturgy-ocean-sunday-1.pdf. © Season of Creation, developed by Norm Habel and the Uniting Church in Australia, Synod of Victoria and Tasmania, 2004, seasonofcreation.com.

107 "We remember and confess . . . ," in "Ocean Sunday," Australian Version 2, Season of Creation, accessed March 17, 2021, https://seasonofcreation.com/wp-content/uploads/2010/04/liturgy-ocean-sunday-2.pdf. © Season of Creation, developed by Norm Habel and the Uniting Church in Australia, Synod of Victoria and Tasmania, 2004, seasonofcreation.com.

108 Frederic and Mary Ann Brussat, "We Are One," Spirituality & Practice: Resources for Spiritual Journeys (SpiritualityandPractice.com), accessed March 16, 2021, https://www.spiritualityandpractice.com/practices/features/view/19952, alt. Used by permission of SpiritualityandPractice.com.

109 From Anne Platt McGinn, "Charting a New Course for Oceans," in *State of the World: A Worldwatch Institute Report on Progress toward a Sustainable Society*, Millennial ed., edited by Lester R. Brown et al. (New York: Norton, 1999), 78, 79, 82, 90, and 95.

110 Anne Rowthorn, "God of Oceans and Estuaries," © 2021 Anne Rowthorn.

111 Michelle L. Torigian, "A World Oceans Day Prayer," MichelleTorigian.com, June 8, 2017, https://michelletorigian.com/2017/06/08/a-world-oceans-day-prayer/, alt. © Michelle L. Torigian. Used by permission.

112 Norman Habel, "Song of the Waters," in *Habel Hymns, Vol. 1: Songs for Celebrating with Creation*, 2004, http://normanhabel.com/wp-content/uploads/2013/09/Hymns-and-Songs-Habel-Hymns-1.pdf. © 2001 Norman Habel.

113 Anne Rowthorn, "May God Who Parted the Waters," © 2021 Anne Rowthorn.

12. MELTDOWN

114 St. Isidore of Seville, "O God, great and wonderful . . . ," alt.

115 Christian Aid, UK, "Loving God, come now and make us . . . ," Christian Aid, accessed March 29, 2021, https://www.christianaid.org.uk/sites/default/files/2020–28/J192308%20CAW%20Autumn%202020%20–%20Prayer%20sheet%20WEB.pdf. Used by permission of Christian Aid.

116 Angelika Dawson for Mennonite Central Committee, BC, "For the People," in "Prayers in Times of Natural Disasters," JesuitResource.org, The Center for Mission and Identity at Xavier University, accessed January 14, 2021, https://www.xavier.edu/jesuitresource/online-resources/prayer-index/prayers-in-times-of-crisis/in-times-of-natural-disaster, alt. Used by permission of Angelika Dawson and Mennonite Central Committee, BC.

117 Diana Macalintal, "A Prayer for after an Earthquake," originally written after the 2010 earthquake in Haiti. © 2010, Diana Macalintal, Liturgy.life. Altered and adapted by Anne Rowthorn. Used by permission.

118 Subrata Ghoshroy, "Fukushima Today: A First-Person Account from the Field and the Conference Table," *Bulletin of the Atomic Scientists*, August 26, 2015, accessed April 28, 2023, https://thebulletin.org/2015/08/fukushima-today-a-first-person-account-from-the-field-and-the-conference-table/. Used by permission of the Bulletin of the Atomic Scientists.

119 "We repent that our lives . . . ," prayer by pastors in Busan, South Korea, in "Christian Activists Pray and Fast to Protest Nuclear Dangers in Busan and Beyond," World Council of Churches, October 22, 2013, accessed January 15, 2021, https://www.oikoumene.org/news/christian-activists-pray-and-fast-to-protest-nuclear-dangers-in-busan-and-beyond. Used by permission of World Council of Churches.

120 Edward Hays, "Candle Prayer at a Time of Need for Another," in Edward Hays, *Prayers for a Planetary Pilgrim* (Easton, KS: Forest of Peace Books, 1988), 216, alt. Excerpted from *Prayers for a Planetary Pilgrim* by Edward M. Hays, © 1989, 2008. Used with the permission of the publisher, Forest of Peace, an imprint of Ave Maria Press®, Inc., Notre Dame, Indiana 46556. www.forestofpeace.com.

121 Joachim Neander, translated by Robert Bridges, "All My Hope on God Is Founded." Public domain.

122 "May God look upon us . . . ," in *Chalice Worship*, edited by Colbert S. Cartwright and O. I. Cricket Harrison (St. Louis: Chalice, 1997), 442, no. 776, alt. Traditional.

13. PANDEMIC

123 Edward Hays, "A Psalm of Longing," in Edward Hays, *Prayers for a Planetary Pilgrim* (Easton, KS: Forest of Peace Books, 1988), 172, alt. Excerpted from *Prayers for a Planetary Pilgrim* by Edward M. Hays, © 1989, 2008. Used with the permission of the publisher, Forest of Peace, an imprint of Ave Maria Press®, Inc., Notre Dame, Indiana 46556. www.forestofpeace.com.

124 Anne and Jeffery Rowthorn, "Loving God, Divine Source of Health," © 2021 Anne and Jeffery Rowthorn.

125 Revelation 21:1–6, 7b from *The Inclusive Bible: The First Egalitarian Translation* (Lanham, MD: Rowman and Littlefield, 2007). © Future Church. Used by permission.

126 Anne and Jeffery Rowthorn, "A Litany for the Dying, the Departed and the Grieving," © 2020 Anne and Jeffery Rowthorn, adapted for general use. This litany is based on Psalm 40:1 and Ecclesiastes 3:1–8. We wrote it as a response to our concern for a dear friend who died alone in a Connecticut hospital, and for his wife and children who, due to hospital regulations, were unable to visit and make their farewells. It broke their hearts. It breaks our hearts.

127 Anne Rowthorn, "Everything Is Beautiful," © 2020 Anne Rowthorn. First written for Anne Rowthorn's personal online journal "Collegeville Journal," May 25, 2020.

128 Patty Jenkins, "Brothers and sisters . . . ," from "Friday Memorial Service," in Religious AF Camp, *A Black Rock Prayer Book*, 47, http://www.ees1862.org/wp-content/uploads/2019/10/A-Black-Rock-Prayer-Book-2019.pdf. Used by permission of Patty Jenkins.

129 Robyn Brown-Hewitt, "Sacred Spirit, you are revealed to us . . . ," in *Celebrate God's Presence: A Book of Services for The United Church of Canada* (Etobicoke, Ontario: United Church Publishing House, 2000), 474, alt. Used by permission of Robyn Brown-Hewitt.

130 Henry Francis Lyte, "Abide with Me: Fast Falls the Eventide." Public domain.

131 "May the Christ . . . ," Almost Daily Prayer, https://www.almostdailyprayer.com/2017/06/celtic-blessing.html. Traditional Celtic blessing.

14. DIVIDED NATION

132 Anne and Jeffery Rowthorn, "Great God of the Universe," © 2023 Anne and Jeffery Rowthorn.

133 C. H. S. Matthews, "True and Enlightened Love of Country," in *Prayers for a New World*, edited and compiled John Wallace Suter (New York: Scribner, 1964), 19, piece 38, language modernized.

134 Marie Hause, "Creator who orders . . . ," © 2023 Marie Hause. Used by permission.

135 Alla Renée Bozarth, "A Litany for Our Common Humanity," alt. © 2022 Alla Renée Bozarth. Used by permission.

136 Lawrence Ferlinghetti, "Pity the Nation," from *BLASTS CRIES LAUGHTER* (09), 23, © 1988, 1998, 2002, 2014 by Lawrence Ferlinghetti. Reprinted by permission of New Directions Publishing Corp.

137 "May it come soon . . . ," from *Windows into Worship*, edited by Ron Ingamells. © 1989 YMCA.

138 Elizabeth Kaeton, "A Prayer to Heal a Divided Nation," in Shiel Catholic Center at Northwestern University order of service for June 10, 2018, Shiel Catholic Center, accessed July 2, 2022, https://sheilcatholiccenter.org/wp-content/uploads/2018/06/06_10_18.pdf. Used by permission of Elizabeth Kaeton.

139 G. K. Chesterton, "O God of Earth and Altar." Public domain.

140 Attributed to Mother Teresa, source unknown.

15. GUN VIOLENCE

141 From Leonardo Boff, *Way of the Cross—Way of Justice*, translated by John Drury (Maryknoll, NY: Orbis, 1982), 126. © Orbis Books. Used by permission.

142 Jean Markey-Duncan, "Today we stand . . . ," from "A Moral Call: People of Faith Confronting the Tragedy of Gun Violence," service of worship from First Unitarian Universalist Society, Burlington, VT, December 13, 2015, on Bishops Against Gun Violence, accessed November 13, 2020, https://bishopsagainstgunviolence.org/wp-content/uploads/2019/09/Moral-Call-Bulletin-FINAL.pdf.

143 Bishops United Against Gun Violence, "O God who remembers . . . ," in Bishops United Against Gun Violence and Episcopal Public Policy Network, "Prayer Service of Lament for Gun Violence" (United Methodist Building Chapel, Washington, DC, March 1, 2019), Bishops Against Gun Violence, accessed November 13, 2020, https://bishopsagainstgunviolence.org/wp-content/uploads/2019/09/BUAGV.EPPN-Prayer-Service-of-Lament-for-GV-3.1-final.pdf. Used by permission of Bishops United Against Gun Violence.

144 Stephen T. Lane, "A Litany in the Aftermath of Gun Violence," Bishops Against Gun Violence, February 28, 2018, https://bishopsagainstgunviolence.org/wp-content/uploads/2019/09/Litany-in-the-Aftermath-of-Gun-Violence-Revised-Feb-2018.pdf. Used by permission of Stephen T. Lane and The Episcopal Diocese of Maine.

145 From Sari Kaufman, transcript of interview by Gunther Peck, "Making Voting Trend with Parkland Student Leader," *Policy 360*, October 30, 2018, accessed May 2, 2023, https://policy360.org/wp-content/uploads/sites/29/2018/10/76-Sari-Kaufman-Transcript.pdf. Used by permission of Sari Kaufman and Gunther Peck.

146 "A Prayer for the Nation in the Midst of Gun Violence," Anglican Fellowship of Prayer, accessed May 13, 2023, https://www.afp.org/index.php, alt. © 2023 Anglican Fellowship of Prayer. Used by permission.

147 René McGraw, OSB, "Loving God, when our world . . . ," © René McGraw, OSB. Used by permission.

148 Carolyn Winfrey Gillette, "God, We Have Heard It," © 1999 Carolyn Winfrey Gillette. All rights reserved. www.carolynshymns.com. carolynshymns@gmail.com. Used by permission.

149 "Within Our Darkest Night." Song from Taizé, © Ateliers et Presses de Taizé, 71250 Taizé, France. Authorized translation from the French text, based on a prayer by Brother Roger of Taizé. Used by permission.

16. RACIAL INJUSTICE

150 Lisa Sharon Harper, "Dearest Jesus, come and sit . . . ," prayer concluding Lisa Sharon Harper, "Martin Luther King Day: Healing Prayer and the Lies We Believe," *Sojourners*, January 13, 2012, accessed May 2, 2023, https://sojo.net/articles/martin-luther-king-day-healing-prayer-and-lies-we-believe. Used by permission of the author. Reprinted with permission from *Sojourners*, (800) 714-7474, www.sojo.net.

151 Catholic Charities USA, "God of justice . . . ," in "Prayer for Racial Healing," Catholic Charities USA, accessed November 15, 2020, https://www.catholiccharitiesusa.org/wp-content/uploads/2018/04/Prayer-for-Racial-Healing.pdf. Used by permission of Catholic Charities USA.

152 Alfredo José Gonçlaves, "Where Do You Come From; Where Are You Going?" in *Prayer without Borders: Celebrating Global Wisdom*, edited by Barbara Ballenger (Baltimore, MD: Catholic Relief Services, 2004), 38, alt. Information sought.

153 From Mahogany S. Thomas, "We Need Faith Narratives That Heal—Now." *Reflections* (Spring 2021), https://reflections.yale.edu/article/making-good-can-faith-repair-world/we-need-faith-narratives-heal-now. Used by permission of the author and Yale Divinity School *Reflections*.

154 Martin Luther King Jr., "O God, our gracious . . . ," prayer closing the sermon "Unfulfilled Hopes," April 5, 1959, Montgomery, AL. King Papers, accessed February 26, 2023, https://kinginstitute.stanford.edu/king-papers/documents/unfulfilled-hopes-0. Reprinted by arrangement with The Heirs to the Estate of Martin Luther King Jr., c/o Writers House as agent for the proprietor New York, NY. © 1959 by Dr. Martin Luther King Jr. Renewed © 1987 by Coretta Scott King.

155 Evangelical Lutheran Church in America, from *Prayer Ventures*, January 2020, alt. © ELCA. Reprinted with permission.

156 James Weldon Johnson, "Lift Every Voice and Sing." Public domain.

17. EDUCATION FOR EXTINCTION

157 Helene Burns, "Today we are invited . . . ," adapted from a prayer by Valerie Kingsbury. Used by permission of Helene Burns.

158 Valerie Kingsbury, "Into this sacred space . . . ," © Valerie Kingsbury. Used by permission.

159 Inspired by Dorothy and Vince Fontaine, "Prayer for the Children of Kamloops Residential School," accessed June 6, 2022, https://mennochurch.mb.ca/res/pub/Manitoba/News/2021-News/Prayer-for-215-Children-of-Kamloops-Residential-School.pdf, alt. Used by permission of Dorothy Fontaine.

160 From Zitkala-Ša, "The School Days of an Indian Girl," *Atlantic Monthly* 85 (1900): 185-94 (pp. 185–87). Hathitrust, https://babel.hathitrust.org/cgi/pt?id=coo.31924079893750&seq=3. Public domain.

161 Reflection © 2023 Pat White Horse-Carda. Used by permission.

162 Woniya Wakan (Holy Spirit) Episcopal Church (Santee-Yankton Mission, Wagner, SD), "A Prayer to Remember the Innocents, June 25, 2022." Used by permission. May be freely copied.

163 Constance Padmore, "Here I am, Lord . . . ," in "An American Lament," Repentance Project, accessed February 16, 2023, https://repentanceproject.org/an-american-lament/. © Arrabon. Used by permission.

164 Words by Gracia Grindal, "Let Flow Our Tears in Grief for This," © 2014 Hope Publishing Company, www. hopepublishing.com. All rights reserved. Used by permission.

165 Lois Wilson, "May the blessing of the God . . . ," in *Chalice Worship*, compiled and edited by Colbert S. Cartwright and O. I. Cricket Harrison (St. Louis, MO: Chalice, 1997), 443, piece 782. From Lois Wilson in *Jesus Christ—the Life of the World*, 102, alt. © World Council of Churches. Used by permission.

18. CIVIL UNREST

166 From Abraham Lincoln, "House Divided" speech (Springfield, IL, June 16, 1858), in *Famous Speeches [of] Abraham Lincoln* (New Rochelle, NY: Peter Pauper, [c. 1935]), 33. Digital Public Library of America, https://dp.la/item/1ca86fc8c80f378ffd703603369523aa. Public domain.

167 "Eternal God, in whose perfect kingdom . . . ," in *The Book of Common Prayer* (New York: Church Hymnal Corporation, 1979), 815, alt.

168 Robert A. Raines, "O God of Miriam and Moses," © Robert A. Raines. Used by permission.

169 Peter J. Scagnelli, "A Christian Prayer for Peace in Our Time," in "Prayers in Times of War and Civil Unrest," JesuitResource.org, The Center for Mission and Identity at Xavier University, accessed October 30, 2020, https://www.xavier.edu/jesuitresource/online-resources/prayer-index/prayers-in-times-of-crisis/in-times-of-war-and-civil-unrest, alt. Information sought.

170 From Pope Francis, *Laudato sì*, accessed December 1, 2022, Vatican.va, 229–31. © Dicastero per la Comunicazione-Libreria Editrice Vaticana. Used by permission.

171 "Almighty God, who has given . . . ," in *The Book of Common Prayer* (New York: Church Hymnal Corporation, 1979), 820, alt.

172 Anna E. Rossi, "Prayer for a New Beginning," in "Prayers for Difficult Times," Grace Cathedral, accessed June 9, 2023, https://gracecathedral.org/prayers-for-difficult-times/. Used by permission of the author.

173 Carolyn Winfrey Gillette, "God of Love, We've Known Division," © 2020 Carolyn Winfrey Gillette. All rights reserved. www.carolynshymns.com. carolynshymns@gmail.com. Used by permission.

174 From Abraham Lincoln, "Second Inaugural Address" (March 4, 1865), in *Famous Speeches [of] Abraham Lincoln* (New Rochelle, NY: Peter Pauper, [c. 1935]), 96. Digital Public Library of America, https://dp.la/item/1ca86fc8c80f378ffd703603369523aa. Public domain.

19. WAR

175 "For Peace," in *A Prayer Book for Australia* (Alexandria, NSW, Australia: Broughton Books, 1995), 202. Used by permission of Broughton Publishing.

176 David Thomas, "A Prayer for Ukraine," in "Prayers for Ukraine," Christian Aid, accessed March 5, 2022, https://www.christianaid.org.uk/pray/prayer-ukraine. Used by permission of Christian Aid.

177 Litany by Creation Justice Ministries: Karyn Bigelow, Avery Davis Lamb, Amanda Robinson, and Helen Smith in "Response to the IPCC 2022 Report," https://www.creationjustice.org/blog/archives/03-2022, 1 March 2022, alt. Used by permission of Creation Justice Ministries.

178 From Olga Aivazovska, "The War in Ukraine: An Eyewitness Account with Olga Aivazovska" (speech, 14th Annual Geneva Summit for Human Rights and Democracy, April 5, 2022), Geneva Summit for Human Rights and Democracy, https://genevasummit.org/speech/the-war-in-ukraine-an-eyewitness-account-2/. Used by permission of the author.

179 "O God, you love justice . . . ," from Masamba ma Mpolo and Mengi Kilandamoko, *Textes liturgiques: Louons Dieu et celebrons la vie*, (Kinshasa, Zaïre: Editions du Cercle Protestant de Pastorale, Spiritualité et Actions Sociales de Kinshasa [CEPROPASKI], 1988). Translated by René Robert, in *In Spirit and in Truth: A Worshipbook* (World Council of Churches, 17th Assembly, 1991), 20. Used by permission of World Council of Churches.

180 "In a Time of International Crisis," Presbyterian Church USA, *Book of Common Worship* (Louisville, KY: Westminster John Knox, 2018), 626. Altered from *The Worshipbook: Services*, © 1970 The Westminster Press. Used by permission of Westminster John Knox Press.

181 Words by Constance Cherry, "When Will People Cease Their Fighting?," © 1990 Hope Publishing Company, www.hopepublishing.com. All rights reserved. Used by permission.

182 "Eternal light, shine in our hearts . . . ," attributed to Alcuin, in *Prayers for a New World*, edited and compiled by John Wallace Suter (New York: Scribner, 1964), 216, no. 469.

20. REFUGEES

183 Anne Rowthorn, "God Made the Dazzling Heavens," © 2022 Anne Rowthorn. Based on Psalm 147.

184 "Dear God of all humanity . . . ," from a service prepared jointly by the Uniting Church in Australia (Assembly Social Responsibility and Justice Committee) and the Asian Church Conference for Human Rights Sunday in Asia, 1996, in *Sinfonia Oecumenica*, edited by Beatrice Aebi et al. (Basel: Im Auftrag des Evangelischen Missionwerks in Deutchland, Hamburg, und der Basler Mission, 1998), 408–10. Used by permission of the Uniting Church in Australia.

185 "As we face this day, O God . . . ," from a service prepared jointly by the Uniting Church in Australia (Assembly Social Responsibility and Justice Committee) and the Asian Church Conference for Human Rights Sunday in Asia, 1996, in *Sinfonia Oecumenica*, edited by Beatrice Aebi et al. (Basel: Im Auftrag des Evangelischen Missionwerks in Deutchland, Hamburg, und der Basler Mission, 1998), 414–16. Used by permission of the Uniting Church in Australia.

186 Alla Renée Bozarth, "All I Had Was Flowers," © 2022 Alla Renée Bozarth. Used by permission.

187 From Alla Renée Bozarth, "A Century Shrinks, History Repeats, Politics Implode," © 2020 Alla Renée Bozarth. Used by permission.

188 Christian Aid, UK, "Merciful God, we pray . . . ," Christian Aid, accessed March 29, 2022, https://www.christianaid.org.uk/resources/worship/we-pray-all-whose-desperation-leads-them-sea. Used by permission of Christian Aid.

189 "For the Human Family," Presbyterian Church USA, *Book of Common Worship* (Louisville, KY: Westminster John Knox, 2018), 630. Altered from *The Book of Common Prayer* (1977). Used by permission of Westminster John Knox Press.

190 Carolyn Winfrey Gillette, "God, How Can We Comprehend," © 1999 Carolyn Winfrey Gillette. All rights reserved. www.carolynshymns.com. carolynshymns@gmail.com. Used by permission.

191 "O Creator and Almighty God . . . ," prayer attributed to an order of service from the Church of Pakistan, in *The United Methodist Book of Worship* (Nashville, TN: United Methodist Publishing House, 1992), no. 524. Based on Annie Johnson Flint, "God Hath Not Promised" (public domain).

21. EXTINCT AND ENDANGERED

192 From Pope Francis, *Laudato sì*, accessed December 1, 2022, Vatican.va, 33. © Dicastero per la Comunicazione-Libreria Editrice Vaticana.

193 Terri MacKenzie, SHCJ, "Call to Prayer" in "Extinction Grieving Prayer," Ecospirituality Resources, accessed August 17, 2022, https://ecospiritualityresources.files.wordpress.com/2014/07/extinction-grieving-prayer-7-16-14.pdf. © Terri MacKenzie, SHCJ, ecospiritualityresources.com. Used by permission.

194 "Prayer of Lamentation," *Spill the Beans* 30 (Lent, Easter and Pentecost 2019), 8 © 2019 Spill the Beans Resources Team. www.spillthebeans.org.uk. Used by permission.

195 Anne and Jeffery Rowthorn, "Litany of the Extinct and Endangered," © 2022 Anne and Jeffery Rowthorn.

196 From "The Grounded Age" by J. Drew Lanham which appeared in the Summer 2022 issue of *Orion Magazine*. Used by permission of *Orion Magazine*.

197 Terri MacKenzie, SHCJ, "Sending Forth," in "Extinction Grieving Prayer," Ecospirituality Resources, accessed August 17, 2022, https://ecospiritualityresources.files.wordpress.com/2014/07/extinction-grieving-prayer-7-16-14.pdf, alt. © Terri MacKenzie, SHCJ, ecospiritualityresources.com. Used by permission.

198 Peter Healy, "Prayer in a Time of Mass Extinction," *Tui Motu: Inter-Islands Magazine*, March 3, 2019, https://hail.to/tui-motu-interislands-magazine/publication/KPXmJQw/article/3wo2rge, alt. Used by permission of Peter Healy.

199 Words by Andrew Pratt, "The Care of Our Planet, the Threat of Extinction," © Stainer & Bell, Ltd. (Admin. Hope Publishing Company, www.hopepublishing.com). All rights reserved. Used by permission.

22. CLIMATE CRISIS

200 Yaryna Serkez, "Every Country Has Its Own Climate Risks. What's Yours?" *New York Times*, January 28, 2021, https://www.nytimes.com/interactive/2021/01/28/opinion/climate-change-risks-by-country.html.

201 Carl Folke, Stephen Polasky, Johan Rockström et al., "Our Future in the Anthropocene Biosphere," *Ambio* 50 (2021), 834, https://doi.org/10.1007/s13280-21-01544-8.

202 The Dalai Lama, in *The Wisdom Teachings of the Dalai Lama*, compiled by Matthew E. Bunson (New York: Penguin Putnam, 1997), 208. From "Humanity and Ecology." © 1988 The Office of His Holiness the Dalai Lama. Used by permission.

203 "Let us give thanks . . . ," prayer attributed to Hawaiian indigenous tradition, in "Nature Prayers for Families," *Bay Witch Musings*, https://nuannaarpoq.wordpress.com/adventures-in-parenting/nature-prayers-for-families/, accessed December 18, 2020, there adapted from "May the earth continue to live . . . ," in *God Has No Religion*, edited by Frances Sheridan Goulart (Sorin Books: Notre Dame, IN, 2005), 125.

204 "A Thanksgiving for Our Country," in Church of the Province of New Zealand, *A New Zealand Prayer Book – He Karakia Mihinare o Aotearoa* (Auckland, New Zealand: William Collins, 1989), 142. © 1989 The Provincial Secretary, The Church of the Province of New Zealand, Box 2148, Rotorua. Used by permission.

205 Jane Deren for Education for Justice and Caritas, Australia, "Climate Justice Prayers of Intercession," adapted in Caritas, Aotearoa New Zealand, *Climate Change Prayer Booklet* for the Just Water: Climate Change in the Pacific series (Caritas, Aotearoa New Zealand, 2017), https://caritas.org.nz/system/files/Climate%20Change%20Prayer%20Booklet.pdf, accessed December 18, 2020, alt. Jane Deren, PhD, Education for Justice. www.educationforjustice.org. Used with permission.

206 From Greta Thunberg, transcript of a speech reported by *The Guardian*, December 10, 2020, https://www.theguardian.com/environment/video/2020/dec/10/greta-thunberg-dismisses-empty-words-in-new-climate-crisis-appeal-video. © 2020 Gripping Films Productions. Used by permission of Gripping Films Productions.

207 "Lord God, we thank you . . . ," in Caritas, Aotearoa New Zealand, *Climate Change Prayer Booklet* for the Just Water: Climate Change in the Pacific series (Caritas, Aotearoa New Zealand, 2017), adapted from a prayer from St Alban's Church in Copenhagen, accessed March 21, 2023, https://link.caritas.org.nz/Climate-Change-Prayer-Booklet.pdf, alt. Used by permission of Caritas, Aotearoa, New Zealand.

208 From Don McKim, "Prayer for the Climate Crisis," *Presbyterian Outlook*, September 9, 2021, updated May 13, 2022, accessed June 14, 2023, https://pres-outlook.org/2021/09/prayer-for-the-climate-change-crisis/. © The Presbyterian Outlook Foundation. Used by permission of Don McKim and *Presbyterian Outlook*.

209 Mary Louise Bringle, "Can You Feel the Seasons Turning," © 2018 GIA Publications, Inc. All rights reserved. Used by permission.

210 Roger D. Knight, "The Grace of God," in *Book of Worship: United Church of Christ* (New York: United Church of Christ Office for Church Life and Leadership, 1986), 114, no. 552. © Roger D. Knight.

23. LAMENT AND HOPE

211 Anne and Jeffery Rowthorn, "Praise to You Holy God of the Universe," © 2021 Anne and Jeffery Rowthorn.

212 Psalm 33:12–15, 18–22 from *The Inclusive Bible: The First Egalitarian Translation* (Lanham, MD: Rowman and Littlefield, 2007). © Future Church. Used by permission.

213 Anne and Jeffery Rowthorn, "Litany of Lament," © 2023 Anne and Jeffery Rowthorn. Inspired by "To Have Hope" by the Missionary Sisters of St. Charles Borromeo, Honduras.

214 Catherine de Vinck, "On My Birthday 99 Years." Used by permission.

215 "All humankind is one vast family . . . ," original attributed to the Book of Remembrance of the Cathedral of St. Paul the Apostle, Los Angeles. Adapted by Anne and Jeffery Rowthorn. Further adapted and expanded for the Fiftieth Interfaith Anniversary of Earth Day, Washington National Cathedral, Washington, DC, April 19, 2020.

216 Anne and Jeffery Rowthorn, "Holy God, Holy and Mighty," © 2023 Anne and Jeffery Rowthorn.

217 Words by Andrew Pratt, "A God of Surprises Beyond Expectation," © 2011 Stainer & Bell, Ltd. (Admin. Hope Publishing Company, www.hopepublishing.com). All rights reserved. Used by permission.

218 Sister Ruth Fox, OSB, "A Nontraditional Blessing" (or "A Mixed Blessing"). Reprinted with permission of Sister Ruth Fox, O.S.B., from the Winter 2014–15 *Abbey Banner*, volume 14, number 3, published by the monks of Saint John's Abbey. © 2014 by Order of Saint Benedict, Collegeville, Minnesota. First published in 1989 in *Living Faith* as "A Mixed Blessing."

EUCHARISTIC PRAYERS

219 Horace L. Allen Jr., "Loving God, Source of All . . . ," from "Eucharistic Prayer C," in The United Church of Canada, *Celebrate God's Presence: A Book of Services for The United Church of Canada* (Etobicoke, ON: United Church Publishing House, 2000), 248–50. © Horace L. Allen Jr. Information sought.

220 Gail Ramshaw, "Triple Praise," in *Pray, Praise, and Give Thanks: A Collection of Litanies, Laments, and Thanksgivings at Font and Table* (Minneapolis: Augsburg Fortress, 2017), 54–56. © 2017 Augsburg Fortress. All rights reserved. Reproduced by permission of the author and Augsburg Fortress.

221 "Eucharistic Prayer 2," in *Enriching Our Worship 1* (New York: Church Publishing, 1998), 60–62. *Enriching Our Worship*, alt. © 1998 Church Publishing Incorporated. Used by permission.

ACKNOWLEDGMENTS

222 Alla Renée Bozarth, "The Awe and Wonder," *Diamonds in a Stony Field: Selected Poems and Prose* (Atlanta: Westwoods, 2022), 547.

INDEX OF BIBLICAL READINGS